CHILTON'S Repair and Maintenance Guide

Truck Campers

ILLUSTRATED

Prepared by the

Automotive Editorial Department
Recreational Vehicles

Chilton Book Company
Chilton Way
Radnor, Pa. 19089
215—687-8200

managing editor **JOHN D. KELLY;** assistant managing editor **PETER J. MEYER;** senior editor, recreational vehicle department, **KERRY A. FREEMAN;** editor **PHILIP A. CANAL;** technical editor **Robert J. Brown;** copy editor **Eric J. Roberts**

CHILTON BOOK COMPANY   RADNOR, PENNSYLVANIA

ML '74 0 1 4 4 3

Library of Congress Cataloging in Publication Data

Chilton Book Company. Automotive Editorial Dept.
  Chilton's repair and maintenance guide for truck campers.

  1. Campers and coaches, Truck—Maintenance and
repair.   I. Title.   II. Title: Repair and
maintenance guide: truck campers.
TL298.C48   1973   629.28'7'6   73-4840
ISBN 0-8019-5744-3
ISBN 0-8019-5852-0 (pbk.)

Contents

629.2876
C 538r

ACKNOWLEDGMENTS

AIR LIFT COMPANY
Lansing, Michigan

AIRSTREAM ®
Jackson Center, Ohio

ATWOOD VACUUM MACHINE COMPANY
Rockford, Illinois

CHEVROLET MOTOR DIVISION, GENERAL MOTORS CORPORATION
Lansing, Michigan

DODGE DIVISION, CHRYSLER CORPORATION
Detroit, Michigan

DUO-THERM ®
La Grange, Indiana

FORD MARKETING CORPORATION
Dearborne, Michigan

GENERAC CORPORATION
Waukesha, Wisconsin

INTERTHERM, INCORPORATED
St. Louis, Missouri

ONAN ®
Minneapolis, Minnesota

OWENS-CORNING FIBERGLAS ® CORPORATION
Lansing, Michigan

RECREATIONAL VEHICLE INSTITUTE, INC.
Des Plaines, Illinois

THE COLEMAN COMPANY, INCORPORATED
Somerset, Pennsylvania

THERMASAN ®
Waukeshia, Wisconsin

THE TIMKEN COMPANY
Canton, Ohio

TOHICKON VALLEY TRAILER CENTER
Quakertown, Pennsylvania

WHEELS AFIELD MAGAZINE
Los Angeles, California

WORTHINGTON CYLINDERS
Columbus, Ohio

Photography by: Joseph F. Pelicciotti

1 · Definition and Classification of Campers

A good discussion of chassis-mount campers and slide-in units should begin with basic definitions in order to prevent possible confusion. Chassis-mount units are usually factory-installed bodies which are bolted to the chassis of larger, chassis-cab trucks. These are self-contained units like motor homes. Pickup campers are quite different, consisting of a slide-in camper unit, which can be removed and replaced by side jacks, and the vehicle itself—which is usually a pickup truck. Unlike a chassis-mount, a pickup unit may be removed so the truck is not restricted to carrying the

Slide-in camper

camper. Camper shells constitute the third category of truck-mounted campers. These are smaller than slide-in units but, like slide-ins, can be removed. They are merely an enclosed covering for the pickup bed.

In the last few years there has been a boom in the sales of pickup units because of this flexibility. The truck owner can use them to transform his basic truck into a home away from home for a weekend or vacation. The shell units have gained their greatest popularity among pickups used in construction or the trades. Valuable tools and other materials can be protected under lock and key in these shells.

Chassis-mount camper

Pickup camper

Camper shell

Campers range in size to accommodate the various sizes of pickup beds and also vary greatly in weight. Naturally the weight of the camper and vehicle must not exceed the maximum gross vehicle weight (GVW) of the truck.

Basic Information

Campers and Pickups

Campers are produced as complete units and their prices depend on the internal components offered. A fully equipped camper will contain the same components as a well-equipped travel trailer, including such accessories as heater, refrigerator, and air conditioning.

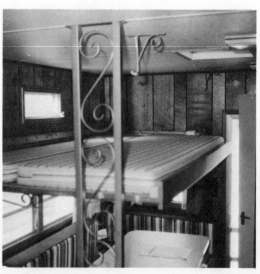

Camper interior

Pickup camper interior

Pickup trucks generally offer a wide range of components. These individual components should be carefully evaluated if you are considering buying a new truck that will, at least partially, be used for hauling a camper unit. The weight and length of the particular camper must also be analyzed to assure compatibility between the truck and the camper. (For further information, see the "Vehicle" section.)

Installation

This procedure is critical. If possible, have a friend (make sure he is a friend) direct you if this is your first attempt at installing the camper. And remember to take it *slowly*.

Remove the tailgate from the pickup, remembering to wrap all the securing screws or bolts and safely store them with the tailgate, while the camper is in use. It is not uncommon to forget where you left the attaching bolts at the end of a season of camping.

Once the tailgate is removed, install the wiring harness connections to the truck. Your owner's manual or the shop manual will include your truck's wiring diagram and the color code of the wires. This will help in locating and matching the camper electrical take-offs. To make certain that the correct connections are made, check the wiring diagram for your camper or ask your dealer.

Jack the camper to the height of the

Removing the tailgate

truck bed—or just a little higher. There are basically two types of camper jacks: those which are permanently attached and those which can be removed. Both types do their jobs well under normal circumstances.

Now that the camper is just slightly above the bed and is secured with at least three jacks (two on one side, one on the other), you can move the truck into position.

NOTE: *If the jacks have tripod bases, keep two legs parallel with the camper body while the other is pointed outward. This will give increased stability and will also keep the legs from being run over by the truck.*

Back the truck slowly so that the bed is centered with the bottom of the camper. Be patient, it may take practice the first time.

CAUTION: *Make sure that the camper is high enough above the bed so that it will clear. If it is not, raise the camper jacks 10 cranks each to gain the correct height.*

Once the truck and the camper are aligned, back the truck slowly under the camper. Make sure that the unit is cen-

tered and that there is no binding. Do not overcorrect once the camper has started onto the bed. If it is not centered, pull the truck out and back in once again.

Installing the unit

Folding the jacks

Removable jack support plate

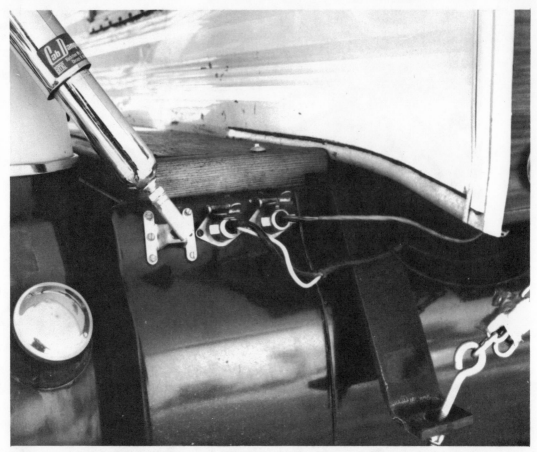

Wiring connections

Camper support mechanism

harness and test the electrical components (taillights, turn signals, back-up lights) for operation.

It is a good practice to recheck the hold-down mechanism after the first 10–20 miles for security and at every 1,000 miles after that. This check should be made more often if the unit is to be used off the road.

Traveling with the Camper

The addition of either a chassis-mount or pickup camper will make your truck noticeably different to drive. You must learn to deal with the differences in order to be truly safe.

Weight (700–1,000 lbs, or even more) is the most obvious difference and wind resistance is another severe problem. Together, these factors cause the engine to

Secure the holding mechanism from the camper to the pickup, making sure that all screws are tight and that all mounting brackets are secure. Connect the wiring

Camper installed on the pickup

work harder to reach and maintain cruising speed. Consequently, more frequent attention must be paid to the engine and drive train components. (See "Vehicle" section.)

The handling of the vehicle will also suffer with the addition of a camper. The center of gravity changes and the added weight makes the unit somewhat harder to handle. Turns will be harder to negotiate because of the tendency to lean into corners. (See "Suspension.")

There are certain components, such as air shock absorbers and anti-sway apparatus, which can be added to make handling a little more predictable. (See the "Vehicle" section.)

There will be wind effect, both side-to-side and front-to-back. The side-to-side is greater and can be most hazardous.

Because of the height of the rig, extreme cross winds can cause the unit to change lanes without warning and make handling extremely difficult. Once again, suspension modifications can be made (which will be discussed later) to alleviate this situation somewhat, but the effect cannot be stopped totally. There is no substitute for knowing your rig.

Checklist for the Road

In order to keep your camping trip from becoming a dismal failure, do as much ad-

vance planning as possible. Experience has shown that the best plan of attack is to make two lists.

The first list will be a permanent list and should include implements that you will always need when using your camper as well as last minute equipment checks that you should always make. This list can then be reproduced or laminated for grease pencil checkoff and it will be routine procedure to run through it before departure.

The second list will be prepared for the special requirements of each trip you plan and will account for weather conditions, purpose of the trip, duration, terrain, etc.

Having these lists will serve two purposes. You will be better prepared each time you use your camper and, in addition, you will have a reference for future planning which will allow you to easily eliminate items that you routinely carry but never use.

Below is a beginning list to which you can add according to your type of camper/vehicle, size of family, purpose of trip, personal preference, etc.

First List

GENERAL

1. A lug wrench which you know fits your vehicle.
2. Spare fuses—one box of each type used in your camper and vehicle.
3. Spare washers for the basin and sink. A leaky washer could cause a pressure failure in the sink.
4. Silicone sealer. This is available in tube or spray and will come in handy on units which are not quite waterproof.
5. Don't forget a can opener.
6. A tie-down chain to secure the camper to the hold down in case of breakage.
7. Three-prong to two-prong adapter plugs, fitted with ground wires.
8. Portable first-aid kit.
9. Holding tank dump hose.
10. Handles for the camper jacks—a screwdriver only means cuts and bruises.
11. Rain gear.
12. Sunglasses for driving.
13. Examine the spare tire to make sure that it is attached securely and that

it contains the specified amount of air. If it is flat, don't just refill it—check for a leak. Also, inspect it for dry rot or other damage.

14. Don't forget the food and snacks. Funny as it may seem, it has happened to the most experienced campers.
15. If the kids are aboard, bring games and amusements to occupy them.
16. Flashlight.

VEHICLE

1. Tool kit.
2. Jumper cables.
3. Extra motor oil.
4. Tow chain (at least ten feet long).
5. Eight feet of plastic siphon tube.

CAMPER

1. Water tank—filled and pressure tested.
2. LP Gas bottles—filled and leak tested.
3. Electrical connections—tight and not frayed.
4. Jacks and handles—secure and operable.
5. Sewage outlet—completely off and capped.

FIRST-AID KIT

1. Aspirin.
2. Antiseptic.
3. Bandaids®.
   a. variety of bandages
   b. compression bandages
   c. wire splints
4. Tweezers.
5. Scissors.
6. Snake bite kit.
7. Baking soda.
8. Adhesive tape.
9. Elastic bandage.
10. Cotton balls.
11. Bandage clips.
12. Safety pins.

EMERGENCY EQUIPMENT

1. Gas lamps and flares.
2. Plastic bucket.
3. Funnel.
4. Emergency food—for two days.
5. Collapsible shovel.
6. Portable radio.
7. Sterno® (4 or 5 cans).
8. Flashlight.

9. Plastic tarp (10 ft x 10 ft).
10. Ten foot tow chain.

Second List

This list will depend upon the particular purpose and conditions of each trip. Be sure to include such items as fishing gear, hunting gear, packing and climbing equipment, foul and cold weather gear, suntan lotion, dog food, mosquito netting and other items peculiar to the nature and destination of your excursion.

Camper Language

CAMPER BODY—A unit designed to slide into a pickup truck or be mounted on a truck chassis. The unit has facilities for sleeping and storage. Some models have "cab-over" design which increases interior room.

CURB WEIGHT (CW)—Weight of the truck with standard equipment, full radiator, crankcase, and fuel tank. This figure should not include either people or the camper body.

GROSS COMBINED WEIGHT (GCW)—Total weight of a fully equipped truck and trailer with cargo, driver and passengers, fuel, water, and any other equipment.

GROSS VEHICLE WEIGHT (GVW)—Total weight of a fully equipped truck with cargo (including the camper), driver and passengers, fuel, water, and any other equipment.

PAYLOAD (PL)—Subtracting a truck's Curb Weight from its GVW rating gives you the Payload allowance. Payload includes the weight of the camper body and contents, driver and passengers.

TRUCK CHASSIS (CHASSIS CAB)—A truck without body but including frame, engine, transmission, driveshaft, springs, axles, wheels and cab.

Camper Weight Distribution

Just the weight of a loaded camper is enough to throw the whole unit out of balance—unless this weight is distributed properly. The object, when loading the camper, is to end up with a perfectly level unit, front to back, and side to side.

A man carrying a 15 ft board would be illustrating the importance of leveling. If he carries it at the center, he balances the board with very little effort. If he carries it at a point away from the center, he is constantly exerting force to keep the board level. Applying this to a camper, we see that most are longer than 15 ft and quite heavy. Balance, therefore, plays a very important role.

The weight of the camper must be supported in the middle of the truck. The next question is: where is the middle? This question can be answered by knowing the dimensions of your pickup just as you knew the length, width and height of the 15 ft board.

The Overall Length (OL) is the distance from the front bumper to the rearmost point on the truck.

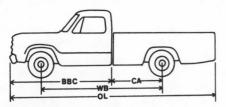

Truck dimensions

The Bumper to Back of Cab (BBC) is the distance from the front bumper to the back of the truck cab.

The Cab Axle (CA) is the distance from the back of the cab to the center point of the rear axle.

The Wheelbase (WB) is the distance from the centerline of the front wheel to the centerline of the rear wheel.

Knowing the truck's dimensions makes the placement of the weight much easier.

One thing is certain: one man would not attempt to pick up our 15 foot board if it weighed 600 lbs. Similarly, the truck should not be loaded beyond its capacity. This means that loaded for the road, the weight of the entire unit should not exceed the maximum GVW for the truck.

ADDING YOUR WEIGHT

Use the following list to check the weight of different camper and truck components.

1. Find the curb weight of the truck. This must include any optional equipment.

2. Record the dry weight of the camper.

3. Add any other weights such as fuel, water, LP gas, etc.

4. Add the weight of the driver and passengers to arrive at the final figure.

If this total weight is below the GVW rating of the truck, everything is fine. If the total weight is above the GVW rating, leave your wife, or some other equipment, at home.

Use the following chart to formulate the approximate weight of the combined unit.

Weight Chart

Item	Approx. Weight (lbs)
1. 4 persons (2 adults, 2 children)	600
2. Food	215
3. Clothing for occupants (4)	100
4. Spare LP gas tank, full	50
5. Water tank (extra) 20 gal.	200
6. Fuel tank (extra) 20 gal.	160
7. Spare battery	25
8. Sporting gear	200
9. Milk (per gal.)	12.4
10. 12, 24–32 oz. bottles	38
11. 24, 6–8 oz. bottles	60
12. Class 1 tow hitch	40
13. Class 11 tow hitch	105
14. Class 111 tow hitch	125
15. Motorcycle (trail)	150–250

DISTRIBUTING THE WEIGHT

Proper distribution of the total truck load (camper plus accessories) depends on the center of gravity (CG) of the pickup. The CG is that point in the truck body at which all other parts of the body exactly balance each other.

In the following illustrations, the shaded area represents the load.

Load over the rear axle

Load proportioned over the two axles

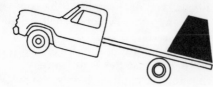

Load to the rear of the rear axle

Center of gravity location

For illustrative purposes the load is "uniform," that is, it weighs the same on both sides of the centerline of the load. In the illustration, the weight is positioned over the rear axle of the truck. This places the entire load on the rear axle. If the load is moved forward, as in the next picture, the weight is distributed between the front and rear axles. However, if the weight should move too far to the rear it will act like a heavy boy on the end of a see-saw —raising the front wheels off the ground.

Generally, most camper bodies are engineered so that the center of gravity is ahead of the rear axle. But some are not, so if you intend to add heavy items behind the rear axle (trail bike, extra LP gas cylinder), this must be equaled by an addition of weight to the front of the unit.

Ask your dealer the location of the center of gravity of your particular camper. Once this is found, it must be located at least 4 in. ahead of the rear axle when the camper is installed.

LOADING YOUR RIG

It is a good practice to pack heavy items first, keeping them on or close to the camper floor. Make certain that these items are well forward of the rear axle. Place light objects on shelves and secure them. Balance the weight as evenly as possible. Trying to control a tailheavy, top-heavy, or lopsided rig is anything but a pleasant experience.

Securing Stored Items

To guard against possible breakage of stored items, make certain that everything is secured. When the camper is moving, there is enough force acting on each component to dislodge it from its place. Use bungie cords (spring loaded tie-down assemblies) or other fastening devices, along with cardboard separators, to prevent damage due to vibration.

WEIGHING THE VEHICLE

If you suspect that the GVW of the pickup has been exceeded after loading, find out for sure. How is this done? Most truck companies have scales, so do grain elevators. Truck scales are often located along major highways. All these will accurately tell the weight of your rig. Once the figure is determined, see if it is within the limits. When weighing the unit also check the weight on the front and rear axles separately. It is possible to be within the total weight limit but still have one axle overloaded.

For example, if the truck GVW rating is 8000 pounds with the front axle rated at 3500 pounds and the rear at 5000 pounds, it is still possible to be within the 8000 pound GVW but have the front axle overloaded with 4200 pounds placed on it. In this case you have two choices: either remove the excess weight from the vehicle or re-position it toward the back of the unit.

Use the following chart to keep a running account of the weight added to the camper and the truck.

Weight Sheet

1. Truck
   a. Trailer Hitch   ‒‒‒‒‒‒
   b. Radio   ‒‒‒‒‒‒
   c. Air Conditioning   ‒‒‒‒‒‒
   d. ‒‒‒‒‒   ‒‒‒‒‒‒
   e. ‒‒‒‒‒   ‒‒‒‒‒‒
   Sub-Total   ‒‒‒‒‒‒ lbs

2. Driver and Passenger(s)   ‒‒‒‒‒‒ lbs

3. Camper Body
   a. Dry Weight   ‒‒‒‒‒‒
   b. Liquid Fuel   ‒‒‒‒‒‒
   c. Batteries   ‒‒‒‒‒‒
   d. Water & Ice   ‒‒‒‒‒‒
   e. Tools and Spare Parts   ‒‒‒‒‒‒
   f. ‒‒‒‒‒   ‒‒‒‒‒‒
   g. ‒‒‒‒‒   ‒‒‒‒‒‒
   h. ‒‒‒‒‒   ‒‒‒‒‒‒
   Sub-Total   ‒‒‒‒‒‒ lbs

4. Equipment and Supplies
   a. Clothing   ‒‒‒‒‒‒
   b. Food and Beverages   ‒‒‒‒‒‒
   c. Kitchen Utensils   ‒‒‒‒‒‒

Weight Sheet (cont.)

d. Toilet Articles   _____
e. Plates, Cups, Glasses, Flatware _____
f. Sheets, Blankets, Towels   _____
g. Miscellaneous   _____
h. _____   _____
i. _____   _____
Sub-Total   _____ lbs

5. Hobby Equipment
   a. Golf Clubs   _____
   b. Guns   _____
   c. Archery Equip   _____
   d. Fishing Equip   _____
   e. Photo Equip   _____
   f. Outboard Motor   _____
   g. Trail Bike   _____
   h. Other   _____
   i. _____   _____
   Sub-Total   _____ lbs

6. Miscellaneous
   a. _____   _____
   b. _____   _____
   Sub-Total   _____ lbs

Total Payload   _____ lbs
Curb Weight of Pickup   _____ lbs
Total Weight (must not exceed
   GVW)   _____ lbs

Single jack assembly

Dual jack assembly

Winterizing and Storage

Certain precautions must be taken to protect your camper against the damage that freezing temperatures can cause. If you plan to store your camper throughout the winter, drain all the water from the plumbing system (i.e., holding tank(s), supply tank(s), waste tank(s), etc.). Otherwise, the expansion of freezing water could crack the pipes.

If you intend to use the camper during the winter months, check with the manufacturer of the individual plumbing components (i.e., tank(s), toilet, shower, sink, etc.) for recommended winterizing additives.

Liquid petroleum gas (LPG) systems should be turned off at the tank. This is also a good time to clean the vents and duct tubes of refrigerators and gas stoves. If these ducts are clogged with soot or debris, they can overheat and break.

Slide-in campers should be stored securely on their jacks in a place where they will not need to be moved. It is best to cover them to guard against the accumulation of dirt.

Chassis-mount campers are similar to motor homes in that they cannot be used without the truck chassis and vice versa. Storage procedures are similar to those outlined in the previous paragraphs for slide-in campers.

2 · The Vehicle

Type

The type of vehicle used for transporting a slide-in camper may range from a foreign mini pickup to a large 1 ton pickup. Gross vehicle weight (GVW), the total weight of a fully equipped and loaded vehicle including the camper, gas, oil, and other camping items, can vary from 4,000 to 10,000 lbs. Therefore, the camper which you buy will depend on the size of the pickup bed and the recommended GVW listed by the vehicle manufacturer.

In recent years, due to the popularity of the pickup camper, manufacturers have introduced pickup-camper packages. These packages include a list of options which the slide-in camper owner would most likely want. They include tie down brackets which make securing the camper to the truck much easier and suspension options which make the camper-truck unit more stable on the road. All these extras are designed to build the truck for the camper so that, as a unit, it will be safe and reliable.

The vehicle section of a chassis-mount camper is received by the camper company as a bare chassis and engine with the cab sometimes included. The company then fastens the camper to the frame of the vehicle. Once again, as in pickup units, the GVWs of the chassis-mount campers vary

Camper tie-down brackets

greatly and provide wide personal choice in selection.

FACTORS AFFECTING THE VEHICLE

Both altitude and climate greatly affect the performance of any vehicle—but especially a truck which must also overcome the added weight of a camper. When you are driving along a road that is new to you, you might easily forget about the adverse effect of increased altitude until you get up around 3,000 ft, even though altitude has been affecting your engine all along.

The feeling is one of sluggishness and lack of power. At 5,000 ft, the engine has lost 14–18 percent of its power. This progression will eventually reach a point where the power loss will be so great that you feel you can walk faster than your rig is moving, even though your accelerator is pushed to the floor. At 10,000 ft, the power loss will be approximately 35 percent of total horsepower.

The problem is caused by the lower oxygen content of air at increased altitudes. If your camper was adjusted for sea level operation, the thin air of mountainous regions will cause an overly rich condition, resulting in smoke, loss of power, and poor gas mileage.

As the altitude increases, inside pressure also increases. Under decreased atmospheric pressures, liquids boil at far lower temperatures which will affect the liquids in the vehicle and in the camper systems. For example, water boils at 212°F at sea level and at 192°F at 11,000 ft above sea level.

If you intend to remain in a high altitude area for an extended period, you should have your truck adjusted for the different conditions. But, if the stay will be only a short one, leave the vehicle as it is because the procedure involves installing new carburetor jets and adjusting the float levels, which takes some time. So, if you are simply passing through a mountain range, you will just have to put up with the temporary inconvenience.

In addition to a power loss, increased altitudes will cause other harmful effects such as percolation of the carburetor, radiator boiling, and carburetor or fuel line vapor lock.

Vapor lock occurs when the fuel pump or fuel line absorbs heat from the engine and causes the liquid gas within these lines to vaporize. Since the fuel pump is made to pump only liquid fuel and not vapors, it pumps nothing and the engine acts as if it is out of gas. This trouble can be avoided if the engine is allowed to idle for a few minutes before it is turned off. Idling will help the engine dissipate heat instead of absorbing it into the fuel system. The only cure is to let the engine cool completely so the gas in the lines will return to a liquid state.

In carburetor percolation, the gas in the carburetor actually begins to boil. The engine will stop running because of an overly rich condition and, once again, the only cure is to let the unit cool and let the gasoline regain its liquid form.

Possibly the most harmful effect of the pressure difference at high altitude is the lowered boiling temperature of the vehicle's brake fluid. This causes the fluid to boil and turn into a vapor which can be compressed, thus causing the brake pedal to go all the way to the floor when the brakes are applied.

Appropriate driving techniques must be used in higher altitudes. When ascending, watch your instrument panel temperature gauges and use the lowest possible gear to avoid lugging the engine, which would cause overheating and those troubles already mentioned.

Brake overheating is common during descent. Although there may be no fade in the brake pedal, there will be no braking action once a brake is overheated. Again, use the lowest possible gear during descent. On vehicles with automatic transmissions, manually shift to a lower gear to keep the rig down to a reasonable rate of speed. The brakes should be applied slightly but constantly. Intermittent heavy braking will heat the brakes and, in some cases, cause the linings to catch fire.

You must certainly stay alert during ascent and descent and the most important point is to be patient. Definitely don't become overly confident.

Climate

Manufacturers design their vehicles to run well in a moderate climate. Modifications may be needed to guard against malfunctions in extreme climates. Such changes as oil coolers, larger radiators, thermostats of a different range, and carburetor adjustment may be used to compensate for the changes. Such options as a heavy-duty radiator, cooling system, transmission, engine, and differential are usually included in camper packages. A transmission cooler can also be ordered. (Installation and discussion of the unit is included in the "Vehicle Transmission" section.)

PERIODIC VEHICLE INSPECTION AND MAINTENANCE

Frequent inspection and timely maintenance is important for any vehicle—but especially so for one which must work as hard as a truck that hauls a camper. Naturally, the factory's recommended service intervals are no longer applicable since they usually don't take the camper into consideration. With the camper in place, the recommended intervals should be cut in half. Although it may seem like a bothersome chore, careful maintenance is a necessity for it assures your family's safety.

Engine Oil and Filter

Oil not only lubricates the moving parts of the engine and protects them from wear, but it also helps to dissipate the heat produced as a by-product of combustion. It is important, therefore, to make sure that the oil is always clean and a proper level is maintained.

Camper owners should follow the viscosity recommendations for heavy-duty use that are specified in the vehicle's owner's manual. Multiviscosity oils are suggested for variable climates. Never mix multiviscosity and single-viscosity oils.

Change the oil filter at least every second oil change. Some people even feel that it is necessary to replace it at every oil change.

Oil takes a tremendous beating during heavy-duty use. It is diluted by acid produced by the engine, and consequently suffers a decrease in its lubricating ability. Oil can fail to perform adequately even if it has not been in the engine for a long time or has not even gotten particularly dirty. The effects of this situation are obvious: worn parts, heat buildup in the engine, and even total engine failure.

Additives are not recommended by most owner's manuals because of the complex chemical construction of the new multiviscosity oils. Instead, careful inspection and regular maintenance are all that is necessary.

Rear Axle Lubricant

The level of the rear axle lubricant should be checked regularly to make sure it meets the level specified in the owner's manual. If the unit is equipped with four-wheel drive, the front axle must also be checked for the proper level. Manufacturers also recommend draining the rear axle lubricant at specified intervals—especially if the unit has heavy-duty use. Check the owner's manual for the recommended intervals and the correct type of lubricant.

If you are losing rear axle fluid, check the housing gaskets and outer axle seals. Leaking fluid will be absorbed into the brake lining and cause a loss of braking power. Overheating of the brakes could also ignite the oil-soaked brake pads and cause a fire.

NOTE: *Keep the vehicle level for an accurate check of the rear axle lubricant level.*

Tune-Up

Too many drivers try to save money by postponing an engine tune-up as long as possible. In reality, this negligence is false economy since worn ignition points and spark plugs or a faulty condenser will cause the engine to misfire. (This is especially true when the extra weight of the camper burdens your truck.) Misfiring will cause excessive engine heat, excessive fuel consumption, a lack of power, and possibly, broken engine parts. A regular tune-up will eventually save lots of money and should be included in your maintenance schedule.

SPARK PLUGS

Reading a spark plug is similar to a doctor taking a patient's temperature. The condition of the plugs can tell, with reasonable accuracy, if the engine is operating correctly. Oil, carbon or other deposits on the plug show some malfunction.

Remove and examine the plugs, comparing them to the illustrations, to locate possible trouble.

Normal operating conditions exist when the plug has no evidence of electrode burning and its body is light tan or gray. Under normal conditions, the plug gap will not increase more than about 0.001 in. every 1,000 miles. When a plug is functioning normally, it can be taken out at 6,000 miles, cleaned, regapped, and replaced in the engine with no ill effects.

Normal condition

Cold fouling takes place when there is an extremely rich fuel-air mixture and it is characterized by a dry, black appearance.

Cold fouled condition

Wet fouling gives much the same appearance as cold fouling, except that the plug shell and electrodes are covered with excess oil.

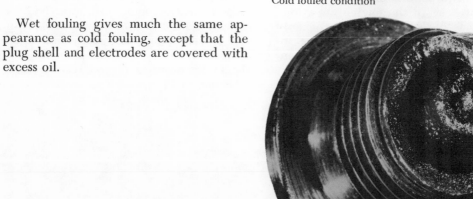

Wet fouled condition

Splash fouling occurs when accumulated deposits in the combustion chamber are loosened and thrown into the spark plug insulator surface.

Splashed fouled condition

Core bridging is a rare condition that occurs when a deposit is thrown against the plug and lodges between the center electrode and the shell of the plug. A bridge is formed between these parts and results in a short circuit.

Core bridged condition

Gap bridging is similar to core bridging except that the deposits bridge the gap between the center electrode and the side electrode, eliminating the air gap which is necessary for proper operation.

High-speed glazing occurs when the temperature of the plug rises suddenly and normal deposits do not have their usual opportunity to be slowly burned from the plug. Instead, they melt and form a conductive coating.

Gap bridged condition

Scavenger deposits, which may be white or yellow, are normal with some brands of fuel and may simply be cleaned off.

Scavenger deposits

Overheating is indicated by a blistered insulator. The insulator will be either white or gray. Spark plugs can be overheated by various engine malfunctions such as overadvanced ignition, cooling system stoppages, and so forth.

Overheated condition

Chipped insulators usually result from improperly adjusting the gap by bending the center electrode. A plug with a chipped insulator should be replaced.

Chipped insulator

Mechanical damage occurs when a foreign object in the combustion chamber damages the spark plug.

Mechanical damage

Reversed coil polarity is best detected by a tune-up oscilloscope, but can be identified by a lack of wear on the center electrode and a semicircular wear pattern on the side electrode. When this condition exists, the primary coil leads are reversed from their proper positions and should be changed.

Reversed coil polarity

BREAKER POINTS

Breaker points should be checked every 5,000 miles or at the intervals recommended in the owner's manual.

When examining the points, check them for alignment with each other and also for any pitting or burning which may be signs of incorrect adjustment.

NOTE: *Under no circumstances should pitted points be filed. Set the gap to the factory specifications and install a new condenser when each new point set is installed.*

ROTOR AND CAP

The rotor and the distributor cap should be examined for wear at every tune-up. Examine the rotor for cracks and the tip contact of the rotor for a burned condition. If either of these are present, the rotor should be replaced.

Examine the interior of the distributor cap for worn contact posts which may suggest rotor misalignment. Also, if there are dirt or other deposits within the cap, they should be removed with soap and water.

Blow the unit dry before installation. If the contact posts are worn, replace the cap.

CARBURETOR, FUEL AND AIR FILTERS

The carburetor should be readjusted with every tune-up. Some newer models have limiter caps on the idle mixture screws which should not be removed. Removal of these units may even void your warranty. Adjust the screws as far as possible with the limiter caps in place. On other models, make adjustments to produce smooth running.

The fuel filter and air filter should be checked regularly—especially if the truck is run in a dusty or dirty area.

Brakes

Stopping ability is the most important aspect of safe camper operation. Most trucks have heavy-duty brakes as standard equipment, some even have finned brake drums and sure-stop metallic linings, but none have brakes so good that the driver can recklessly exceed his Gross Vehicle Weight (GVW).

All brakes are subjected to tremendous stress under normal conditions. It would, therefore, be terribly dangerous to overload your rig with a camper that is too large, or is, itself, overloaded. Once the GVW is exceeded, handling and stopping are adversely affected and the strain will be so great that some type of failure is almost inevitable.

NOTE: *It is not possible to raise the GVW of a vehicle with air shock absorbers, stabilizer bars, or larger tires or wheels. This limit is determined at the factory and considers the strength of chassis metal, wheels, and suspension components.*

Watch the amount of brake lining left on your vehicle. For the recommended inspection intervals, consult your owner's manual, under "heavy-duty usage."

The brake lining must never wear enough to permit the metal bonding surface or the lining rivets of the brake shoe to contact the drum on shoe units, or the rotor on disc systems. This could cause irreparable damage to the drum or rotor which both cost a great deal to replace.

Wheel Cylinders

Leaking wheel cylinders are the most frequent cause of brake failure. Since the advent of the dual brake system, there is not as great a chance of wheel cylinder failure as there used to be, but the possibility still exists.

The wheel cylinders should be checked when the brake lining is examined. Look for brake fluid leaking from the dust covers over the end of the cylinders. If there is no fluid evident, pull back the dust covers and check to see if fluid has leaked past the interior plungers.

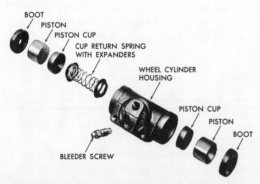

BOOT
PISTON
PISTON CUP
CUP RETURN SPRING
WITH EXPANDERS
WHEEL CYLINDER
HOUSING
PISTON CUP
PISTON
BOOT
BLEEDER SCREW

Exploded view of a wheel cylinder (Courtesy of Chevrolet Motor Division G.M. Corp.)

If any leakage is evident, service the cylinder immediately. The best service is to replace the cylinder rather than rebuild it. If one leaky cylinder is found, the others may be on their way. It is a good practice, especially on vehicles like campers where stopping a heavy load is important, to replace all the cylinders at one time just to gain peace of mind knowing that no wheel cylinder failure could cause disaster.

Cooling System

The cooling systems of chassis-mount campers are especially engineered to cope with the heavy load. Pickup campers, however, are engineered only to the recommended GVW of the pickup. In both cases, the system must be kept clean and free from blockage at all times. For smooth engine operation under these high-load conditions, the cooling system must be in top condition.

Some type of summer-winter antifreeze should be kept in the system throughout the year. These solutions contain rust inhibitors which keep rust and sludge from forming on the inside of the cooling system and causing a blockage. Consult your owner's manual or dealer for antifreeze recommendations.

Wheel Bearings

The wheel bearings on both chassis-mount and pickup campers must be sufficiently lubricated at all times. Consult your owner's manual for the type of lubricant to be used and the required intervals for lubrication. Use the time period listed under "heavy-duty usage."

The bearings must be lubricated with the correct lubricant because the heat dissipating characteristics and lubricant heat ranges vary. For example, a new lithium based grease is required for the disc brake system wheel bearings. Ordinary grease will melt.

Some chassis-mount or tandem-wheel pickups may have rear axle bearings which must be lubricated in the same manner as the front wheel bearings. Do not forget to service these bearings.

Make sure the bearings are packed correctly; they will fail otherwise. If the bearing lubricant runs dry, the speed of the turning wheel and the pressure of the weight will weld the bearings to the spindle. This will cause irreparable damage to the spindle and require replacement.

After packing the bearing, make sure that the spindle nut is torqued to the proper specifications. This is extremely important since this torque (on disc brakes) positions the caliper in relation to the rotor. Also make certain that a new cotter pin is used after the adjustment is completed.

BEARING DIAGNOSIS

The following section will help diagnose bearing failure and its causes. Use it to recognize bearing failure and to decide whether replacement is necessary.

Treat a used bearing in the same manner as a new one. Always work in a clean area with clean tools. Remove all outside dirt from the bearing housing before installation and make certain that the bearing is packed correctly before installation.

CAUTION: *Never spin a bearing which is not packed with lubricant as this will cause bearing wear and certain failure.*

Wheel Bearing Troubleshooting Chart

Condition	Cause	Serviceability
General Wear	Wear on races and rollers caused by fine abrasives.	Clean all parts and check seals. Install new bearing if old one is rough or noisy.

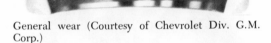

General wear (Courtesy of Chevrolet Div. G.M. Corp.)

Condition	Cause	Serviceability
Step Wear	Wear pattern on roller ends caused by fine abrasives.	Clean all parts and check the seals. Install new bearings if the old one is rough or noisy.

Step wear (Courtesy of Chevrolet Div. G.M. Corp.)

Wheel Bearing Troubleshooting Chart (cont.)

Condition	Cause	Serviceability
Indentations	Surface depressions on races and rollers which are caused by foreign particles.	Clean all parts and check the seals. Install a new bearing if the old one is rough or noisy.

Indentations (Courtesy of Chevrolet Div. G.M. Corp.)

Condition	Cause	Serviceability
Galling	Metal smears on the roller ends due to overheating from improper lubricant or overloading.	Install a new bearing. Check the seals and be sure the proper lubricant is used.

Galling (Courtesy of Chevrolet Div. G.M. Corp.)

Condition	Cause	Serviceability
Etching	Bearing surfaces appear gray or gray black with related etching.	Install a new bearing and check the seals. Be sure the proper lubricant is used.

Etching (Courtesy of Chevrolet Div. G.M. Corp.)

Wheel Bearing Troubleshooting Chart (cont.)

Condition	Cause	Serviceability
Cage Wear	Wear around the outside diameter of the cage and the rollers caused by foreign material and poor lubrication.	Clean all parts, check the seals, and install a new bearing.

Cage wear (Courtesy of Chevrolet Div. G.M. Corp.)

Condition	Cause	Serviceability
Fatigue Spalling	Flaking of the surface metal due to fatigue.	Clean all parts and install new bearings.

Fatigue spalling (Courtesy of Chevrolet Div. G.M. Corp.)

Condition	Cause	Serviceability
Stain Discoloration	Stain discoloration ranging from light brown to black, caused by lubricant break-down or moisture.	Reuse bearings if the stains can be removed by light polishing and no overheating exists. Also check the seals for damage.

Stain discoloration (Courtesy of Chevrolet Div. G.M. Corp.)

Wheel Bearing Troubleshooting Chart (cont.)

Condition	Cause	Serviceability
Heat Discoloration	Discoloration can range from faint yellow to dark blue due to overload or lubricant breakdown. Softening of the races or rollers can also occur.	Check for softening of parts by drawing a file over suspected areas. The file will glide easily over hard metal, but will cut soft metal. If overheating is evident, install new bearings. Check seals and other parts.

Heat discoloration (Courtesy of Chevrolet Div. G.M. Corp.)

Condition	Cause	Serviceability
Brinelling	Surface indentations in the race caused by rollers under impact load or vibration while the bearing is not rotating.	If the old bearing is rough or noisy, install a new bearing.

Brinelling (Courtesy of Chevrolet Div. G.M. Corp.)

Condition	Cause	Serviceability
Bent Cage	Due to improper handling	Install a new bearing.

Bent cage (Courtesy of Chevrolet Div. G.M. Corp.)

Wheel Bearing Troubleshooting Chart (cont.)

Condition	Cause	Serviceability
Misalignment	Outer race misaligned	Install a new bearing and be sure the races and bearing are properly seated.

Misalignment (Courtesy of Chevrolet Div. G.M. Corp.)

Condition	Cause	Serviceability
Cracked Inner Race	Crack due to improper fit, cocked bearing, or poor bearing seats.	Install a new bearing and be sure it is seated properly.

Cracked inner race (Courtesy of Chevrolet Div. G.M. Corp.)

Condition	Cause	Serviceability
Frettage	Corrosion due to small movement of parts with no lubrication.	Clean all parts and check seals. Install a new bearing and be sure of proper lubrication.

Fretting (Courtesy of Chevrolet Div. G.M. Corp.)

Wheel Bearing Troubleshooting Chart (cont.)

Condition	Cause	Serviceability
Smears	Metal smears due to slippage caused by poor fit, improper lubrication, overloading, or handling damage.	Clean parts. Install a new bearing, and check for proper fit and lubrication.

Smears (Courtesy of Chevrolet Div. G.M. Corp.)

Hold-Down Assemblies

There are many varieties of hold-down assemblies to fasten the camper to the pickup. Most consist of a turnbuckle arrangement which fastens to brackets on the camper and to the outside of the pickup.

Once the camper is in place, the hold-downs must be secured to keep the camper body from shifting from side to side and front to back. Installation procedures, explaining the positioning of the camper hold-down mechanism, are included with the camper. Refer to these when positioning the anchor bolts into the pickup body.

Tires and Wheels

Use good tires on both pickup and chassis-mount campers. Recapped, worn, or dry rotted tires should never be used. Traveling on badly worn tires is dangerous. Also remember to check the wear on the front tires for possible front end misalignment.

Follow the manufacturer's recommendations for ply rating when you choose a replacement tire. Some people may feel that by increasing the ply rating, they can also increase the GVW limit, and can pile in more "necessities," but that is not true. GVW is almost always a constant which considers the tensile strength of the truck's suspension and other, similarly complicated, details.

Wheels normally require little or no maintenance but it is smart to examine around the wheel stud holes for hairline cracks which may come from rough driving.

The wheel/tire combination is one of the most important parts of the camper unit. Keep the tires inflated to the proper pressure and make certain that the wheels are in good condition, with no bent edges. Have the front end aligned if there are signs of excessive front tire wear.

Vehicle Safety

Check out the entire rig before each trip. If you aren't up to it yourself, find a qualified mechanic.

After you get underway, you'll also have to remember to allow for your camper's peculiarities and/or limitations because it certainly won't drive like the family sedan. For one thing, it's big. You must be especially careful when parking or passing. And, since it is so heavy, you must allow more time to slow down. For safety's sake, and since it is so easy to misjudge, allow

1½ truck lengths for every 10 mph and never tailgate.

Obey speed limits. They are posted for your safety. Also reduce speed under hazardous conditions such as fog, rain, snow, or sleet.

Actually this safety section is nothing more than common sense. Of course you should obey posted speed limits and reduce your speed at night and when it is foggy or raining. Ultimately, you should know your rig, its capabilities and its tendencies. If you do, the unit should always be totally predictable.

Vehicle Components

OVERLOAD SPRINGS

Overload springs are added to the truck to prevent sag under load and to raise the rear of the vehicle.

Extra spring leaves should be installed by a mechanic since the process is involved and requires the removal of the differential U-bolts as well as the separation of the existing units. Some companies market helper springs which work the same way but are somewhat easier to install.

Extra springs naturally make the ride stiffer and somewhat less pleasant so they should not be added if they are not really necessary.

LIMITED-SLIP DIFFERENTIAL

Since rear axle traction is the key to stability and forward movement, the transfer of torque from the engine to the differential should be complete.

Most conventional differentials are nonlocking. While both rear wheels are on dry ground, the driving torque is distributed evenly. Under slippery conditions, when one of the rear wheels is on a dry surface and one is on a slippery surface, the conventional or "open" differential tends to transfer the torque of the engine to the wheel with the least resistance: the wheel on the slippery surface. This results in loss of traction.

The limited-slip differential (known under different names to different vehicle manufacturers) incorporates a clutching mechanism into the differential.

Again, the natural tendency is for the torque to be transferred to the wheel on the wet surface, but instead, the clutches engage and transfer the torque to the wheel which is on dry ground, regaining traction.

If you plan to do a lot of camping where there is snow or sand, you will find this option well worth its price.

If you aren't sure whether your camper has a locking differential, jack up the rear so both rear wheels clear the ground. Make certain that the unit is supported securely. Spin either tire forward and watch the movement of the other tire. If the tire turns in the same direction as the one you are turning, the differential is a limited slip type unit; if the tire turns in the reverse direction, the axle is the "open" type.

REAR AXLE RATIOS

The rear axle ratio is an important factor in the pulling ability of the unit. Chassis-mount campers have relatively fixed loads and their best axle ratios can be determined at the factory.

Our concern in this section is the rear axle ratio of pickup trucks that will be used with slide-in campers.

The ratio itself is the relationship between the number of turns of the driveshaft and the number of turns of the drive axles. If the truck is equipped with a 3.73 differential, the driveshaft will turn 3.73 times for each time the drive axles turn once.

To recommend an axle ratio for a specific model truck is not easy. The size and horsepower of the engine must be considered along with the weight of the camper and the kind of terrain over which the unit will be driven. A lower ratio differential (numerically higher, as 4.11:1) would possibly be good for a camper with a smaller engine; it would offer more low end torque. A higher ratio (numerically lower, as 3.08:1) would be better for a truck with a larger engine.

To find your differential ratio, check the numbers on the differential housing with your dealer and he will look up the ratio for you. It is important to know your differential ratio, especially if your truck wasn't purchased with camping in mind, because an incorrect ratio can cause problems.

If the ratio is too high, the clutch will

have to be slipped to get the unit moving initially, causing clutch wear. If the ratio is too low, the top speed of the rig will be lowered and the engine will run above the acceptable rpm range at highway speeds.

TRANSMISSIONS

Manual

For years the manual transmission has been considered superior for towing. Closer examination of the clutch has recently shown some of its disadvantages, however.

A clutch is designed to provide positive engagement and a limited amount of slip to get the load moving. When the pickup is fitted with a large camper and a few hundred pounds of home necessities, the clutch must be slipped greatly in order to start the truck in motion. This results in a short clutch life. Once moving, engagement is positive.

Automatic

With the advent of modern, three speed automatic transmissions, old wives' tales about automatics have fallen by the wayside. In fact, trailer towing and camper packages from most manufacturers recommend automatic transmissions.

Older automatics probably lived up to the fears of camper drivers because the truck itself was not designed for camping. Either the differential had an incorrect ratio or the transmission was not designed for heavy use. To function correctly, the vehicle must be geared to handle the heavy load. See the rear axle section.

The advantage of the automatic transmission is that torque may be applied gradually without any slipping. This gradual starting procedure allows the slow transfer of torque to the rear wheels and minimizes traction loss and wheel spinning.

TRANSMISSION OIL COOLERS

Transmission oil coolers are sometimes offered in manufacturer's camper packages. Because of the extra load on the pickup, there is an increase in transmission heat. This heat is transferred to the transmission oil. If the oil is allowed to become too hot, it will change its chemical composition or burn. Valve bodies can then become clogged and the transmission won't

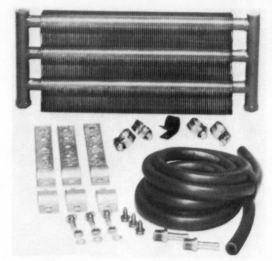

Transmission cooler components (Courtesy of Ford Motor Corp.)

operate as efficiently as it should. Serious damage to the transmission can result.

Break-down of transmission fluid is indicated by a burned smell and discoloration of the oil. Burned transmission fluid is dark brown or black compared to its normal bright red. Burned fluid will have a distinctive odor. The fluid will "cook" in stages and produce sludge and varnish which clogs the transmission. An internal leak in the radiator oil cooler could contaminate the transmission fluid too. Check the fluid for any of the above conditions by removing the transmission dipstick and holding it against a piece of paper towel. Examine the stick closely for small pieces of sludge or varnish. Even a small piece can clog the transmission valve body. If any particles are evident, immediately drain the transmission, clean the filter screen, and install new fluid.

Never install an oil cooler assembly in front of the truck's radiator; this will cut the cooling capacity of the radiator and will cause overheating.

Proper driving techniques can also lower the transmission temperature. Do not lug the engine. (Lugging is the condition whereby an increase in fuel to the engine fails to produce a noticeable increase in engine speed.) Instead, shift the vehicle into a lower gear. This should be done whether the vehicle is equipped with a manual or an automatic transmission. With the automatic, this procedure has to be done manually. Don't wait for the transmission to downshift itself. This re-

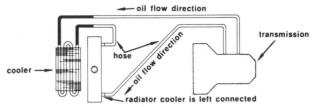

Transmission cooling system (Courtesy of Ford Motor Co.)

duces the heat from the transmission by increasing the mechanical efficiency of the torque converter. Engine cooling is also increased due to higher fan and water pump rpm.

WHEELS AND TIRES

There are many variables in choosing the right wheels and tires. What type of driving will you be doing? Over what type of terrain? Will you be traveling at high speeds for long periods of time? Will there be snow or mud where you will be going? Will you be traveling off the road very often? Will your tires be subjected to extremely high road temperatures?

The following list describes the characteristics of different types of tire construction.

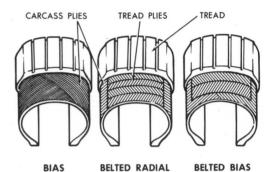

Tire composition

1. The conventional bias construction consists of overlapping cords running from one wire bead to the other at an angle, usually about 30°. Alternate plies run across at an opposite angle. This construction affords both sidewall and tread-surface rigidity.

2. The radial tire differs in construction from the conventional bias tire in that the cords run from bead to bead at an angle of 90° to the direction of travel. There is a belt around the tire inside the tread. This construction gives the tread great rigidity and the sidewall great flexibility. The belts restrict the amount of "squirm" when the tread comes in contact with the pavement and this improves tread life.

3. The bias-belted construction consists of angled cord, similar to the conventional bias tire, but also belts under the tread, as in the radial ply tire. This type of construction gives rigidity to the tread and the sidewall of the tire. Tread life is improved over the conventional bias tire but the objectional feeling of instability sometimes found in the flexible sidewalls of radials is eliminated.

NOTE: *Moving up to more tire plies will make the ride stiffer. Do not use a stiffer tire than is necessary.*

WARNING: *Heavy-duty suspensions are recommended for radial tires. These tires will "cup" and wear unevenly on a*

On-off road tire design

standard suspension. Never mix radial ply tires with any other type on the same axle. If oversized tires are to be installed, install wider rims to fit the increased width of the tires.

Tread Design

Tread design should also be considered when selecting tires for your vehicle. Will you be driving off the road frequently? Will you be driving at high speed for long periods of time? A combination of both or strictly one or the other? Very few people drive strictly off the road, but for those who do, a heavy-duty tread design is best for traction and the protection of the tire. For highway use, choose a moderate tread design which will run quietly, deliver

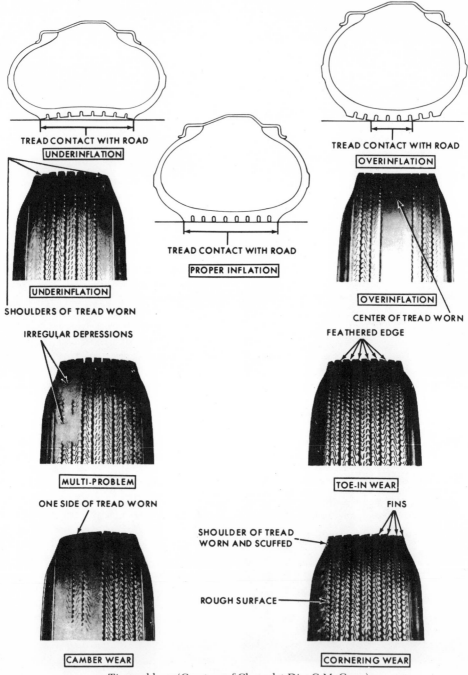

Tire problems (Courtesy of Chevrolet Div. G.M. Corp.)

good mileage, and stay cool while running at high speeds. There are designs for both on-road and off-road use which will stay cool and quiet.

NOTE: *Radial tires are not recommended for off-road use because the stiff tread will cause the sidewalls to bulge when the tire contacts a surface object. When this occurs, the sidewalls become susceptible to cuts and punctures.*

Tire Pressure

Tire pressure plays an important part in the stability of the truck. Low or uneven pressure can cause hard handling, erratic braking, and possibly, swerving.

Frequently check the tire wear pattern. If the tire is wearing unevenly on both outer edges and the center is not wearing, it is underinflated. Increased wear at the center of the tire with no wear at the edges shows overinflation.

Check the tire pressure at least weekly and DO NOT trust the tire pressure gauges in gas stations. These are often found to be incorrect by as much as 10 psi. Buy your own.

AIR SHOCK ABSORBERS

Air shock absorbers are a relatively new development. They look much like conventional shock absorbers from the outside but the inside contains an internal power piston which expands and contracts with air pressure.

Air shocks were first used on race cars because their suspensions had to be altered from race to race to compensate for the changes in track conditions. For campers and heavily laden trucks, they can be a welcome solution to the problem of rear-end sag.

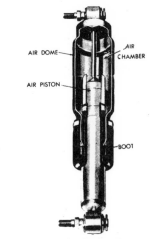

Internal view of air shock absorber

CAUTION: *The maximum pressure range is listed on the casing of these shocks. Do not exceed this pressure.*

Air shocks can help to attain a level riding height. This level state is important for correct weight distribution in braking and steering.

NOTE: *Do not raise the rear end of the vehicle so high that the front weight distribution is incorrect. This will result in erratic handling and increased tire wear.*

CAMPER PACKAGES

Large truck manufacturers have recently assembled camper packages to afford the best handling and performance for pickup campers.

These packages include larger front and rear springs, a front or rear sway bar, larger tires with wider rims, larger engines, and lower differential ratios. Most manufacturers publish brochures to tell which models are capable of carrying

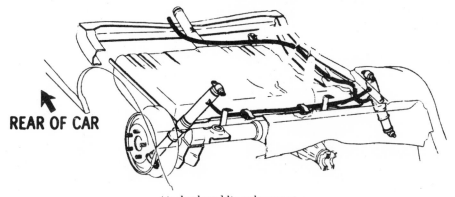

REAR OF CAR

Air shock and line placement

what size campers. They also include required and recommended optional equipment which will make carrying the camper
much easier. You should consider each
component carefully and in light of your
camper's intended use.

SIDE MIRRORS

Because of the extended width of
campers, many manufacturers include side
view mirrors with their camper packages.
If they are not included, buy a pair immediately.

Side mirrors are the only means of di-
recting the camper since the interior rear
view mirror is unusable.

These mirrors come in various sizes and
extensions so pick the one suited for your
rig and your needs. Also, if you are not ac-
customed to driving with the camper or
the mirrors, practice backing and turning
with the unit. The best place for this is an
empty supermarket parking lot on a Sun-
day morning or any other time when there
are no parked cars to interfere. Back into a
parking space using the parking lines on
the pavement and see how close you come

to perfection. Naturally, take it *very*
slowly.

The mirrors should be adjusted to a
comfortable driving position so that shifting in the driver's seat is not necessary.
Once this is set, tighten the mirrors securely.

Beside the conventional flat mirrors,
convex mirrors are available for wide
angle viewing.

Flat and convex mirrors

CAB DAMPERS

Cab dampers are shock absorbers which
are attached from the cab to the pickup
bed to guard against flex of the truck body
when the camper is installed.

There are many different models and
types available and their recommended attaching points differ. So check with the
manufacturer before installing the units.

Considering the great amount of weight
in the bed of the pickup, there can be a severe amount of flexing between the bed
and the cab—especially when the unit is
used off-road. To offset this, the dampers
are installed. It has been proven that they
greatly reduce this flex by leveling the
shock in the same manner as an automotive shock smooths the ride of a car.

Pickup camper with mirror assembly

Damper

Dampers can also be positioned from the overhead sleeping area to the front of the truck to eliminate front-to-back movement of the camper as a result of sudden stops.

FOUR-WHEEL DRIVE

A four-wheel drive (4WD) pickup with a chassis-mount camper is an ideal vehicle if you like off-road camping. A camper with 4WD offers greatly increased traction over the conventional two-wheel drive machine.

The only disadvantage of older 4WD units is a stiff ride on open roads. Modifications to newer models ease that stiffness somewhat.

4WD units also offer special equipment for slide-in campers.

The popularity of 4WD began with people who found that surplus jeeps offered a new form of recreation in off-road driving. Manufacturers gradually entered the 4WD market and currently offer a wide variety of these vehicles.

A 4WD vehicle is basically the same as a conventional, two-wheel, rear-drive model but has been combined with a front-drive axle with a power drive to pull the vehicle while the rear axle pushes. The addition of the front drive axle doubles the traction. If you plan to do much off-road driving and/or camping—especially in sand or snow—4WD may be just right for you.

BRAKES

There are two types of brake systems: drum brakes and disc brakes.

The drum brake system has been used for years. It is composed of a lining which

is either bonded or riveted to a half-moon shoe. There are two shoes under each brake drum. When the brakes are depressed, the shoes expand and contact the inner surface of the brake drum, causing the vehicle to stop.

The disc brake system works in a slightly different manner. It consists of a rotating disc (rotor) assembly which is vented for air cooling and is attached to the suspension and linked with the wheel through the spindle. The brake pads are situated on either side of the disc. When the brakes are applied, the pads press in against the rotor disc, slowing the vehicle.

The disc brake system is more efficient because it resists brake fade and brake failure due to water logging. Unfortunately, discs are available, only as an option, for the front wheels on most trucks.

Shoe brakes (Courtesy of Chevrolet Div. G.M. Corp.)

Disc brake assembly

Camper Recommendations

	8 ft Shell Tops 1000 lbs & under	8–9½ ft (Not Cabovers) 1000 to 1500 lbs	9–10½ ft Cabovers 1500 to 2000 lbs
Chevrolet/GMC	Model C10/1500 with 5400-lb GVW	Model C10/1500 with maximum GVW package. 6000 lbs	Model C20/2500 with 7500-lb GVW
Dodge	Model D-100 with 5500-lb GVW	Model D-200 with 6200-lb GVW	Model D-200 with 7500-lb GVW
International	Models 1010, 1110 with maximum GVW package	Model 1210 with 6100-lb GVW	Model 1210 with 7500-lb GVW
Jeep	J-2600 model	Model J-2600	Model J-4700
Ford	Model F-100 with 5500 GVW	Model F-250 with 6200-lb GVW	Model F-250 with 7500-lb GVW

	9–10½ ft Cabovers 2000 to 2600 lbs	Cabovers 10½–11 ft 2000 to 2600 lbs	Cabovers 10½–12 ft 3200 to 4200 lbs
Chevrolet/GMC	Model C20/2500 with 8200-lb GVW	Model C30/3500 with the proper GVW package	Model C30/3500 with dual wheels and proper GVW package
Dodge	Model D-200 with 9000-lb GVW	Model D-200 with 9000 GVW	Model D-300 chassis-cab with the proper GVW package (This unit is used only for chassis mounts)
International	Model 1210 with 8200-lb GVW	Model 1310 with 9000-lb GVW	Model 1310 or 1510 chassis-cab with the proper GVW package (This unit is used only for chassis mounts)
Jeep	Model J-4800	J-4800 Note—Gross weight should not exceed 8000 lbs	Not recommended
Ford	Model F-250 with 8100-lb GVW	Model F-350 with 8350-lb GVW	F-350 with 9500-lb GVW

Manufacturer's Specifications for Slide-In Units

JEEP

Model	Commando	J-2000	J-4000
GVW (lbs)	3900–4700	5000–6000	5000–8000
Box length (in.)	66	84	96
Engines	232, 258 (6) 304 V8	258 (6) 304, 360 V8	258 (6) 360 V8
Axle ratios	3.73 : 1 4.27 : 1	4.09 : 1 4.88 : 1	4.09 : 1 4.88 : 1
Transmissions	3 speed manual 4 speed manual	3 speed manual 4 speed manual automatic	4 speed manual automatic

Minimum Recommendations for Slide-In Campers

Model	Commando	J-2000	J-4000
Up to 2000 lbs	304 V8 with automatic trans	All models	All models
2000–3500 lbs	304 V8 with automatic trans 4700-lb GVW pkg	304 V8 with automatic trans	All models
3500–5000 lbs	Not recommended	360 V8 with automatic trans 6000 GVW pkg	Automatic trans or 4 speed manual 6000-lb GVW pkg
5000–8000 lbs	Not recommended	Not recommended	Automatic trans or 4 speed manual 8000 GVW pkg

Manufacturer's Specifications for Slide-In Units (cont.)

INTERNATIONAL

Model	1010	1110	1210	1310	1310 (Chassis-Cab)
GVW (lbs)	4800 5500 opt	4800 5500 opt	6100– 8200	7000– 16,000	7000– 9000
Box length (in.)	78 or 96	78 or 96	78 or 96	78, 96 or 108	None
Engines	The 258 (6) and the 304, 345, and the 392 V8's are available on all models				
Axle ratios	3.07 : 1, 3.31 : 1, 3.54 : 1, 3.73 : 1, 4.09 : 1, 4.10 : 1		3.54 : 1, 3.73 : 1, 4.10 : 1, 4.30 : 1, 4.56 : 1, 4.87 : 1		
Trans- missions	All models are available with a 3 speed manual, two 4 speed manuals, two 5 speed manuals and a 3 speed automatic.				

Minimum Recommendations for Slide-In Campers

Model	1010	1110	1210	1310	1310 (Chassis-Cab)
Up to 2000 lbs	All models	All models	All models	All models	All models
2000– 3500	304 V8, 4 speed manual or auto- matic trans		304 V8, 4 speed manual or auto- matic trans		NA *
3500– 5000	345 V8 with 4 speed or automatic transmission should be used in all models.				
Over 5000	Not recommended for either		392 V8 with 4 or 5 speed manual or automatic		

* NA—Not Applicable

Manufacturer's Specifications for Slide-In Units (cont.)

CHEVROLET (GMC)

Model	C-10/1500	C-20/2500	C-30/3500
GVW (lbs)	4900–6000	6400–8200	6600–10,000 *
Box length (in.)	78–96	96	96
Engines	250 (6) 307, 350, 454 V8s	250 and the 292 (6) also 307, 350, and 454 V8	
Axle ratios	3.07 : 1, 3.40 : 1, 3.73 : 1, 4.11 : 1	3.73 :1, 4.10 : 1, 4.56 : 1, 5.13 : 1	
Trans-missions	3 or 4 speed man or Turbo Hydra-Matic	3 or 4 speed manual or the Turbo Hydra-Matic	

Minimum Recommendations for Slide-In Campers

Model	C-10/1500	C-20/2500	C-30/3500
Up to 2000 lbs	350 V8, 4 speed man or Turbo Hydra-Matic 3.73 : 1 axle and 2000 lbs rear springs. Also power brakes	Same as C-10 only with 4.10 : 1 axle	Same as C-20
2000–5000	Same as above requirements	Same as above requirements	Same as C-20
Over 5000	Same requirements as 2000–5000 lbs except that the 454 with the Turbo Hydro-Matic trans is recommended	Same as the 2000–5000 lbs except that the 454 with the Turbo Hydro-Matic trans or 4 speed manual is recommended	Same as C-20

Manufacturer's Specifications for Slide-In Units (cont.)

FORD

Model	F-100	F-250	F-350 (Super Camper)	F-350
GVW (lbs)	4550–5500 max. for 4-wd.	6200, 6900, 7500 8100 (NOTE: 7700 is max. for 4wd)	8350 to 9500	6600, 8000 single rear wheels; 8300, 9000, 10,000 with dual
Box length (in.)	81 or 96	96	96	108
Engines	240 (6) 302, 360, 390 V8	300 (6) 360, 390 V8	360, 390 V8	300 (6) 360, 390 V8
Axle ratios	3.25 : 1, 3.50 :1, 3.70 : 1	3.54 : 1, 3.73 : 1, 4.10 : 1	4.10 : 1	3.73 : 1, 4.10 : 1, 4.56 : 1
Trans- missions	3 or 4 speed manual or Cruise-O-Matic	3 or 4 speed manual or Cruise-O-Matic	Cruise-O-Matic	4 speed manual Cruise-O-Matic

Minimum Recommendations for Slide-In Campers

Model	F-100	F-250	F-350 (Styleside)
Up to 2000 lbs	5000 lb min. GVW, 360 V8 w/auto trans and light duty tow package	All models with 360 V8 and light tow pkg	All models w/360 V8, auto trans and light duty tow pkg
2000– 5000 lbs	5500 lb min. GVW w/360 V8, auto trans, 3.50 : 1 axle also HD tow package *	Same equipment as used in the F-100	Same equipment as the F-250
Over 5000	Not recommended	Same equipment as the 5000 lb F-100 but w/7500 GVW, and 4.10 : 1 axle ratio	Same equipment as the F-250 over 5000 lb but including 390 V8

* HD Tow Package—This includes: larger radiator, 7 wire wiring harness, heavy duty flasher, transmission oil cooler, heavy duty battery, 55 amp alternator, ammeter and oil pressure gauges and a pair of extended mirrors.

Manufacturer's Specifications for Slide-In Units (cont.)

DODGE

Model	D-100	D-100(*)	D-200	D-200(*)	D-200(**)	D-300	D-300(**)
GVW (lbs)	4600 to 5500	5000 to 5500	6200 to 9000	6200 to 9000	6200 to 9000	6600 to 10,000	8600 to 10,000
Box length (in.)	78 or 96	78 or 96	96	96	78 or 96	108	none
Engines	All series models are available with 225 (6) or the 318, 360, and 400 V8s						
Axle ratios	2.94 : 1, 3.20 : 1 3.55 : 1, 3.90 : 1		3.54 : 1, 4.10 : 1			4.10 : 1, 4.56 : 1, 4.88 : 1	
Transmissions	3 speed manual, two 4 speed manuals, LoadFlite automatic trans					Two 4 speed manuals and LoadFlite automatic trans	

Minimum Recommendations for Slide-In Campers

Model	D-100	D-200	D-300
Up to 2000 lbs	All models using towing pkg plus heavy duty rear springs	All models using towing pkg	All models using towing pkg
2000–7000	The limit for the D-100 is 6000 GVW with 360 V8, towing pkg, 3.20 : 1 or 3.55 : 1 axle, 3 speed automatic or 4 speed manual transmission and heavy duty tires	All models using the towing pkg, 2700 lb rear springs, 360 V8 with a 3.54 : 1 axle or higher for over 4000 lb GVW. Also the 3 speed automatic or the 4 speed manual is recommended with heavy duty tires	Same components as D-200 except 4.88 : 1 axle, and the 3600 lb rear springs are recommended

*—Club cab
**—Crew cab

3 · Fuel and Heating

The Liquid Petroleum Gas System

Most chassis-mount and slide-in campers use liquid petroleum gas (LPG) for heating, cooking, lighting, and refrigeration. It affords the mobility and the convenience of bottled gas.

In this system, the gas is stored in pressurized containers which are usually mounted on the rear of the camper, or else in a compartment which is sealed from the inside of the trailer, but vented to the outside. The gas feeds the appliances through lines which are usually ½ in. copper tub-

LP gas cylinder

LP gas refrigerator

ing with brass connectors, or possibly sweat fittings (on the older models).

FUELS

Butane and propane are the two basic fuels for campers. Both produce a clean, even flame which is ideal for cooking and heating. One of the most beneficial properties of these gases is that both can be stored in a closed container, and can be converted, by pressure, from a liquid to a gas. The gas remains at the top, inside the container, while the liquid gas is on the bottom. As the gas is used, the pressure within the cylinder reduces, causing the vaporization of the liquid in the bottom. This converts it to a gas. The container is empty when all of the liquid gas has vaporized and all of the upper gas has been used.

It has been proven that a gallon of butane produces more heat than a gallon of propane. Butane, however, has a higher "freezing" point than propane which means that the vaporization quality by which it changes from a liquid to a gas is stopped and it remains a liquid. Consequently, butane cannot be used where the temperature is below 32° F. Since propane has a lower freezing temperature, it is sometimes mixed with butane to lower the overall freezing temperature. Propane can also be used alone—especially where the climate is extremely cold.

Never allow your camper's gas tank to empty completely since air will enter the lines, requiring them to be bled before the system can be reused. Different campers will consume different quantities of gas, depending on how many gas-operated accessories there are, the size of the tank, and so forth. You'll just have to keep a close watch on your supply.

To make all this easier, you can fit the tank with a gauge. This will make it possible to measure exactly how much gas the

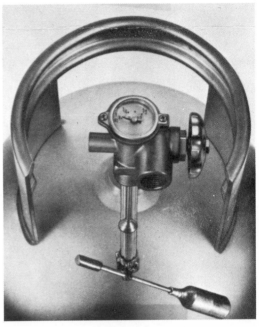

Cylinder gauge (Courtesy of Airstream Corp.)

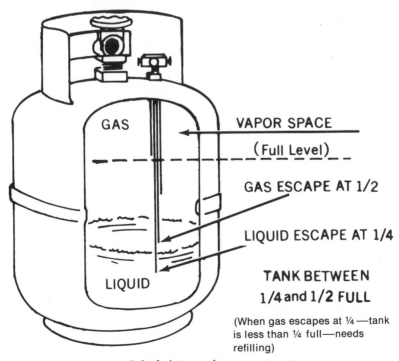

GAS

VAPOR SPACE

(Full Level)

GAS ESCAPE AT 1/2

LIQUID ESCAPE AT 1/4

LIQUID

TANK BETWEEN
1/4 and 1/2 FULL

(When gas escapes at ¼ —tank
is less than ¼ full—needs
refilling)

Cylinder's internal components

cylinder contains. Otherwise, the weight of the tank compared to a full cylinder is the easiest way of measuring. It is also possible, however, to note the condensation marks on the outside of the container which mark the upper level of the gas.

CAMPER GAS FLOOR PLAN

Some of the gas line connections may become loose, due to road vibration, possibly causing leaks. It is necessary, therefore, to know the floor plan of the camper's LPG system so the location of the fittings and connections will be known and accessible for a check. Your camper owner's manual or your dealer's service manual should contain the floor plan for your LPG system.

The only other way to learn the layout of the LPG system is to find out yourself by tracing the lines through the camper to the various appliances. This may be hard and time-consuming, but it is necessary in order to avoid leaks which could cause an explosion.

GAS RACK ASSEMBLY

There are many types of support racks for the gas bottles; most consist of a level base plate with an extended support rod which has a forked top extending out. The collar of the cylinder slides into the fork and the middle of the cylinder is restrained by a belt around the middle and is secured by a wing nut, or some other locking mechanism.

LPG Tank Removal and Replacement

The tank may be removed by first removing the regulator assembly from the tank(s). Loosen and remove the hold-down assembly and slide the tank from the support plate. To install the new tank, reverse the removal procedure.

LPG REGULATOR

The regulator on the bottled gas containers is an important addition to the fuel system. The valve governs the amount of pressure that the gas appliances receive from the bottled gas container. The regulator is adjusted to 11 in. of water column at the factory and should not be tampered with by the novice. (This can become rather complicated but, basically, the reference to 11 in. of water column indicates a specific method of measuring and main-

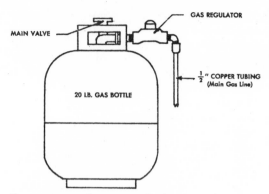

Connections to the LP gas cylinder

taining sufficient—but not excessive—gas pressure throughout the system.) If the regulator is found to be faulty, a new unit should be installed by a qualified person.

To remove the regulator from the tank system, close the supply valve on the tank(s). Remove the connecting lines—with the regulator attached—and remove the regulator by releasing the coupling.

Some units are equipped with an automatic gas regulator and two gas cylinders that use one regulator which is connected to both tanks. While the on-off valves on both tanks are open all the time, the regulator draws from only one tank at a time.

One tank is used until it is empty and then the regulator automatically switches to the full tank. The valve of the empty tank is turned off so it can be removed and recharged, after which it is reinstalled by connecting the output line from the regulator to the tank, and then opening the valve.

Testing the LPG System for Leaks

If there is evidence of a leak (sound or smell), immediately begin tests; the probability of a fire or explosion is great. Make frequent checks of the connections, fittings, and outlet valves to lessen the possibility of a leak.

Since LP gas is clean and odorless after it is refined, federal law requires that it be combined with Mercaptan which has a distinctive odor. If there is a leak, the smell of the Mercaptan should be evident and the degree of the odor will indicate the seriousness of the leak. If there is a great amount of odor, the gas should be turned off at the tank, all windows and doors of the trailer should be opened, and the trailer should be evacuated until the smell subsides. Mix a combination of soap and water in solution. This will be the leak finder. *Never use a match or flame to find a gasleak.* Once it is safe to enter the trailer, coat the suspected fittings with the solution, have an assistant turn on the gas, and watch for air bubbles at the fittings. Use this procedure for all leaks.

Since LP gas condenses on the floor of the camper (it is heavier than air), it is possible to sweep the gas from the camper with a broom or a large piece of cardboard. You might look comical doing this, but it really works.

The average gas line is ½ in. tubing with flaired-fitting endings. Leaks are usually caused by these fittings coming loose because of vibration. Tightening the fitting securely should cure the leak. Do not overtighten the fitting, however, because the flaired end could be damaged beyond repair. All that is necessary is a snug fit. Never use any sealing compound on a flaired fitting; this will only clog the line and distort the seating surface of the connector.

NOTE: *If the leak in the system cannot be found, turn off the gas at the tank and take the rig to your service center to have the leak located immediately.*

HEATING SYSTEM

Some type of heater is a necessity for year-round camping in colder climates. Camper heaters (usually an option) are

Exterior heater vent

Position of the heater near the floor of the camper

Wall-mounted heating unit (Courtesy Intertherm Corp.)

small units, constructed as an integral part of a lower cabinet assembly, and they run on LP gas.

The operating principles of all heaters are very similar. Outside air is drawn

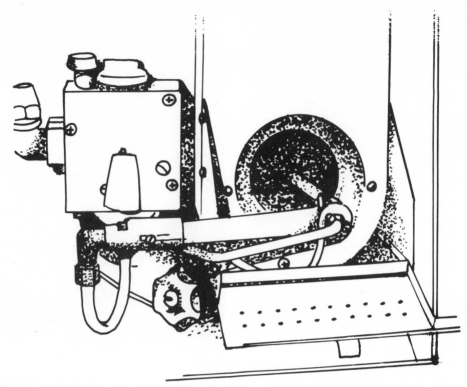

Burner assembly

through an air intake and flows into the sealed burner chamber. This air is combined with gas at the venturi port where combustion takes place. The heat from the main and pilot burners is vented to the outside through the combustion vent. Most units have a sealed combustion system which prevents the products of combustion from entering the living area.

Once the heat is produced by combustion, it must be distributed throughout the camper to be effective. This is accomplished by the air circulation system. An internal fan moves cooler air from the interior of the camper across the surfaces of the heat exchanger which warms the air. This air is then channeled out of the heating ducts and into the trailer. There is usually a filtering device at the air intake to free the trailer air of dust and dirt particles.

The Pilot

Most heaters use a thermocouple. When heat is applied to a thermocouple, it generates a small amount of electricity which is used to power an on-off shut-off valve for the main gas jet. This is used as a safety procedure. If the pilot goes out, the heat is removed from the thermocouple and it cools, thus stopping the electrical charge. When the charge stops, the circuit to the shut-off valve is broken and the main jet is turned off. This system eliminates possible explosion due to accumulation of gas in the absence of a pilot flame.

To light a thermocouple system, turn the selector to pilot and depress the starter button. Light the pilot with an extension wick, keeping the starter button depressed

HEAT EXCHANGER

LIGHTER DOOR

THERMOSTAT (OPTIONAL)

MAIN BURNER AND PILOT GAS CONTROL

MOUNTING AREA FOR AIR CIRCULATOR (OPTIONAL)

Heater components

for 10 seconds. Release the button; the pilot should stay lighted. On automatic start models, depress the starter button and push the starting mechanism button to light the pilot.

Gas Burner Adjustment

The gas burner for the heater is usually located behind a lower access panel. On some of the newer models, it may be slightly harder to locate. If the pilot light is out, light it and observe the color and intensity of the flame. The flame should ideally be blue with a small yellow tip. On older units, there is an air adjustment screw which can be used to adjust the intensity and composition of the flame. The newer units are not adjustable. If the flame is erratic, you must clean the orifice of the burner with a toothpick or alcohol. Never use metallic implements to clean the orifice or it may be enlarged. The best answer is to replace the orifice.

Blower Assembly

The blower assembly, inside the heating unit, circulates the inside air over the heated coils to heat the camper. This is a completely closed system; there is no mixture of the burner gases (which heat the heating coils) and the air (which is moved by the blower around these coils to heat the camper).

When the thermostat indicates that heat is needed, the blower motor engages immediately. As the blower motor is in mo-

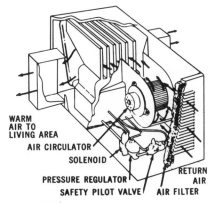

WARM
AIR TO
LIVING AREA
AIR CIRCULATOR
SOLENOID
PRESSURE REGULATOR
SAFETY PILOT VALVE
RETURN
AIR
AIR FILTER

Heater air circulation

tion, the microswitch trips and channels gas to the main burner where it is lighted by the pilot. Some units, after they have run for a long time, tend to keep the blower motor running even though the burner is in the "off" position. This removes the remaining gases which may be trapped in the heat exchangers.

Heater Maintenance

The heater assembly should require no maintenance other than periodic cleaning of the burner ports to remove any soot which might have been deposited. If you encounter serious difficulty, consult the manufacturer.

Make certain that the vent to the outside of the camper is free of soot; it could clog and cause serious damage. Check this vent frequently.

4 · Air Conditioners and Generators

Air Conditioners

Air conditioners are available for both pickup and chassis-mount campers. They are mounted on the roofs of these units because there is no safe and convenient alternative location. To leave them hanging from windows or protruding from the body is obviously hazardous. An air conditioner mounted on the side of a camper can greatly alter the weight distribution and center of gravity of the rig, adversely affecting its driving characteristics.

Mounting the air conditioner in the center of the roof allows the cooling capacity of the unit to be fully realized. The cool air flow can be directed to the front or rear of the camper without any restriction that would be caused by cabinets or fixtures. A roof-mounted air conditioner is able to cool more efficiently without affecting the stability of the camper.

INSTALLATION AND GENERAL MAINTENANCE

Installation of an air conditioning unit is an involved procedure which should only be attempted by a qualified mechanic. This procedure includes installing the roof-mounted unit and the interior venting system.

The system is made up of the exterior unit and the interior duct work.

The intake and exhaust vents are on the inside of the trailer. The intake vents contain air filters which should be cleaned periodically to prevent clogging.

Most units also have a thermostat. This thermostat cycles the air conditioner on and off to maintain the air in the camper at the predetermined temperature.

Aside from the routine maintenance procedures which are outlined in the owner's manual, there is not much maintenance work the average owner can do to his camper's air conditioning system. Special tools and knowledge are needed to replace most parts.

The air conditioning system is pressurized; if a leak develops, it must be attended to immediately or the system will be contaminated. The following paragraphs explain the basic operation of the air conditioner and offer a general idea of what the trouble might be if the unit doesn't work properly.

Roof-mounted air conditioning unit (Courtesy of Duo-Therm Corp.)

THEORY OF AIR CONDITIONING

The basis of an air conditioning system is the removal of heat from an enclosed area. Heat is absorbed when a liquid is changed to a vapor. (This is demonstrated by placing a drop of alcohol on the back of your hand. Because the alcohol is highly unstable, it will evaporate quickly and absorb the heat from your hand.) Simple evaporation is, therefore, shown to be the simplest form of evaporation.

If we had an unlimited supply of refrigerant and cost was not a factor, evaporation would be a successful refrigeration system. We could continuously boil off the refrigerant and continue to absorb heat by using the refrigerant only once. Unfortunately cost is a factor, so the refrigerant must be recyclable. By using an entirely closed system, the coolant may be liquified and reused. Air passing over the outside of the evaporator coils will be cooled as its heat is absorbed by the refrigerant which is evaporating inside. Outside air removes the heat picked up by the refrigerant when it passes through the condenser coil.

The basic components of a refrigeration system are:

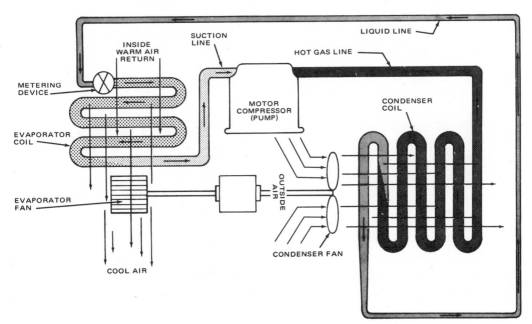

Internal components of air conditioning unit (Courtesy of Intertherm Corp.)

1. An evaporator cooling coil
2. A suction line
3. The compressor
4. The condenser coil
5. The liquid line
6. A metering device

To understand the air conditioning system completely, these basic premises must be accepted.

1. Heat will flow only from a relatively warm substance to a relatively cool substance.

2. A refrigerant exists as both a gas and a liquid at the same temperature, if it is at its "boiling point." A refrigerant at its boiling point will boil (vaporize) and absorb heat from its surrounding air, if the air is warmer than the refrigerant. A refrigerant at its boiling point will condense and become liquid, losing heat to the surrounding air if it is cooler than the refrigerant.

3. The boiling point of the refrigerant rises as the pressure rises, and falls as the pressure falls.

The Refrigeration Cycle

1. The compressor compresses the refrigerant vapor, increasing its temperature and pressure, and forces it along to the condenser coil.

2. At the condenser coil, air, which is cooler than the refrigerant, passes across the outside of the coil and absorbs some of the refrigerant's heat. The refrigerant temperature will decrease until it is cooled to its saturation point. In this state, the vapor will condense to a liquid.

3. The liquid, which is still under high pressure from the compressor, flows through the small liquid line to a metering device. The metering device can be either an expansion valve or a capillary tube.

4. The high-pressure liquid refrigerant is forced through the metering device, reduced in pressure, and then expands into the evaporator. Under this low-pressure condition, the liquid begins to boil until it is in a vapor state.

5. During this change from a liquid to a gas, the refrigerant absorbs heat from the air flowing across the outside of the coil. The air, losing its heat, becomes very cool, thus cooling the room.

6. The evaporated and heat-laden refrigerant at low pressure is then drawn into the compressor through the suction line. The whole cycle is then repeated.

The half of the system under high pressure is called the "high side." The other

Air conditioner components (Courtesy of Airstream Corp.)

1. Compressor	5. Motor mounting hardware	9. Capacitor terminals protector
2. Compressor mounting hardware	6. Cover panel assembly	10. Junction box
3. Condenser	7. Cap assembly	11. Plug and wiring harness assembly
4. Blower assembly	8. Run capacitor	

Air conditioner components (Courtesy of Airstream Corp.)

12. Fan guard
13. Fan blade
14. Venturi panel
15. Fan motor
16. Motor support bracket
17. Mounting hardware for fan and motor assembly

18. Potential relay
19. Start capacitor
20. Wire harness assembly
21. Control box cover
22. Blower housing

23. Blower inlet rings
24. Blower wheel
25. End capacitor assembly
26. Evaporator coil

half of the system, which is under low pressure, is called the "low side."

AIR CONDITIONER MAINTENANCE

1. Clean the air filters regularly. These are usually made of fiberglass or foam rubber and can be washed in soap and warm water. The air conditioner should never be operated without the filters in place.

2. Keep the evaporator coil clean. If the passageways between the fins are plugged, carefully brush down the inner surface with a soft brush or cloth to remove surface lint. Be careful not to flatten or damage the fins. If the coil is clogged to any depth, it may have to be steam-cleaned.

3. If your air conditioner is equipped with an evaporator drain tube, check it regularly. If it seems to be clogged, blow through the tube to open it. If this doesn't work, run a wire through the drain tube to open it. Check to see if the tube is kinked or bowed; make certain that it is sloping toward the drain outlet.

4. Keep the condenser coils clean by using the same procedure as outlined in procedure no. 1.

5. Keep the louvers or screening on the outside cover free from leaves, paper, and other foreign material which would restrict the flow of air into the unit.

Troubleshooting Chart for Air Conditioners

Condition	Cause	Remedy
1. Compressor does not start	1. Open switch	1. Close switch
	2. Fuse blown	2. Replace fuse
	3. Broken connection	3. Check circuit and repair
	4. Overload circuit breaker stuck	4. Wait for a time and check current
	5. Frozen compressor or motor bearings	5. Replace the compressor
	6. Open circuit in compressor stator	6. Replace the compressor
2. Compressor starts; motor will not get off starting windings; high amperage and rattle in the compressor	1. Improper wiring	1. Check the wiring against the wiring diagram
	2. Low line voltage	2. Check the line voltage and correct
	3. Relay defective	3. Replace relay if defective
	4. Run capacitor defective	4. Replace capacitor
	5. Compressor motor starting and running windings are shorted	5. Replace compressor
	6. Starting capacitor weak	6. Check capacitor; replace if necessary
	7. Tight compressor	7. Replace compressor
3. Compressor will not start; hums and trips on overload	1. Improperly wired	1. Check wiring against diagram
	2. Low line voltage	2. Check line voltage and correct
	3. Starting capacitor defective	3. Replace the capacitor
	4. Relay contacts not closing	4. Check to see why the contact points are not closing; replace if defective
	5. Compressor motor is grounded or has open winding	5. Replace compressor
	6. Tight compressor	6. Replace compressor
4. Compressor starts and runs but short-cycles	1. Low line voltage	1. Check line voltage and correct
	2. Additional current passing through overload protector	2. Check wiring diagram. Check the fan motors for wrong connections
	3. Run capacitor defective	3. Check capacitance and replace
	4. Compressor too hot; inadequate motor cooling	4. Check refrigerant charge
	5. Compressor motor windings are shorted	5. Replace compressor
	6. Overload protector defective	6. Check the current. If the unit does not recycle, replace the compressor
	7. Compressor tight	7. Replace compressor
	8. Discharge valve defective	8. Replace compressor
5. Compressor short cycles	1. Dirty air filter	1. Replace
	2. Refrigerant charge low	2. Recharge system
	3. Restricted capillary tube	3. Replace
	4. Dry condenser	4. Clean condenser
	5. Compressor valve leaks	5. Replace compressor
	6. Overload protector cutting out	6. Check current. If the unit does not reset, replace the compressor
6. Unit operates too long or continuously	1. Shortage of refrigerant	1. Fix leak and recharge
	2. Control contacts frozen or stuck closed	2. Clean points or replace
	3. Insufficient air or dirty condenser	3. Check for clogging and correct

Troubleshooting Chart for Air Conditioners (cont.)

Condition	Cause	Remedy
6. Unit operates too long or continuously	4. Air-conditioned space is poorly insulated or excess load 5. Compressor valves are defective 6. Restriction in refrigerant system 7. Filter dirty 8. Air is bypassing the coil or service load	4. Replace with larger unit 5. Replace compressor 6. Find and correct 7. Clean or replace 8. Check return air and keep doors closed
7. Camper temperature too high	1. Refrigerant charge low 2. Control set too high 3. Capillary tube plugged 4. Iced or dirty coils 5. Unit too small 6. Insufficient air circulation 7. Capillary tube does not allow enough refrigerant 8. High and low pressures approaching each other; compressor valves are defective 9. Low line voltage 10. Dirty air filter 11. Dirty condenser	1. Check for leaks and recharge 2. Reset control 3. Repair or replace 4. Defrost or clean 5. Replace with larger unit 6. Correct air circulation 7. Replace tube 8. Replace compressor 9. Decrease load in line or increase wire size 10. Replace 11. Clean condenser
8. Starting capacitor open, shorted, or burned out	1. Relay contacts are not operating properly 2. Improper capacitor 3. Low voltage 4. Improper relay 5. Short-cycling	1. Clean contacts or replace 2. Check for proper rating and voltage 3. Find the cause 4. Check the parts list and replace 5. See section under "Compressor starts but short-cycles"
9. Running capacitor open, shorted, or burned out	1. Improper capacitor 2. Excessive high line voltage	1. Check for proper rating 2. Line voltage must be in proper range
10. Relay is shorted or burned out	1. Line voltage is too low or high 2. Incorrect running capacitor 3. Relay loose 4. Condenser air is off	1. Find trouble and correct 2. Replace with correct capacitor 3. Tighten the relay 4. See "Compressor starts but short-cycles"
11. Condenser pressure too high	1. Air in system 2. Incorrect running capacitor 3. Relay loose 4. Short-cycling	1. Purge the system 2. Clean condenser 3. Discharge some refrigerant 4. Check condenser motor connections
12. Condenser pressure too low	1. Refrigerant charge too low 2. Compressor discharge or suction valves defective 3. Entering temperature to evaporator is low	1. Fix leak and recharge 2. Replace compressor 3. Raise temperature
13. Frosted or sweating suction line	1. Capillary tube passes excessive refrigerant	1. Check the size and bore of the capillary tube

Troubleshooting Chart for Air Conditioners (cont.)

Condition	Cause	Remedy
13. Frosted or sweating suction line	2. Evaporator fan not running 3. Overcharge or refrigerant	2. Repair or replace 3. Correct to the right charge
14. Hot liquid line	1. Low refrigerant charge	1. Fix leak and recharge
15. Frost on capillary tube	1. Ice plugging capillary tube	1. Apply hot wet cloth to capillary tube. If suction increases moisture is present
16. Noisy unit	1. Tubing rattle 2. Fan blade causing vibration 3. Refrigerant overcharged. Liquid refrigerant in the compressor 4. Loose parts or mountings 5. Motor bearings worn 6. Leak of oil in the compressor	1. Fix so it is free of contact 2. Check for a bend 3. Check for correct charge; replace capillary tube 4. Fix and tighten 5. Replace motor 6. Replace compressor

Generators

BASIC THEORY

Generators operate by passing an electrical conductor through the lines of force of a magnetic field causing current to flow. The direction of the flow is dependent upon the direction of the mechanical movement and polarity of the magnets.

All the generators which are used in campers generate alternating current (AC) only. For discussion purposes, this type will be referred to as an "alternator." The other type is known as a "generator." The main mechanical difference between the two is the physical placement of the magnetic field.

In a generator, the magnetic field is sta-

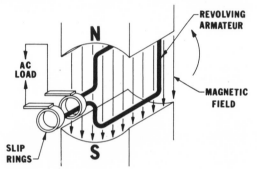

Internal construction of a generator (Courtesy of Generac Corp.)

tionary and the current is taken from the revolving armature. In an alternator, the magnetic field revolves and the AC (alternating current) is generated in the fixed stator. This alternator is basically the

Generator (Courtesy of Onan)

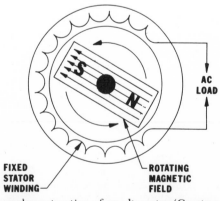

Internal construction of an alternator (Courtesy of Generac Corp.)

Generator access door

same type that is installed in cars. The AC is transformed into DC (direct current) by diodes. Campers generally use AC generators to power AC appliances but in some instances the AC is converted to DC by rectifier diodes.

The relationship between current flow and magnetism is the basic principle by which all electric motors, alternators, generators, and transformers operate. Any conductor that has current flowing through it has a magnetic field at right angles to the direction of the flow. If a laminated core of iron is wrapped with a coil of wire and current is put through the wire, a magnetic field will be created. The end of the core where the current enters the coil will become the north end of the field and the end from which the current leaves the coil will become the south end of the magnetic field. The larger the amount of current which flows through the windings, the greater the magnetic field.

As previously stated, current flowing through a conductor creates a magnetic field. Conversely, the lines of force of the magnetic field passing through a conductor cause current to flow in that conductor. The current flowing in the primary windings, called the exciting current, must vary in amplitude to produce an expanding and collapsing magnetic field in the secondary

winding where the current leaves the mechanism. The current on the secondary is called induced current. Once again, a current is produced by either moving a conductor through magnetic lines of force or moving the magnetic lines of force through a conductor.

These are the basic principles by which all alternators or generators work. The explanation given is a highly simplified version of a complex process. Do not attempt any repairs to your generator unless you have the knowledge and experience to service the unit.

MAINTENANCE

Some routine maintenance procedures are given in the following paragraphs. These can be performed by almost anyone with a basic knowledge of mechanical procedures and a limited supply of tools.

Any generator installed in a camper unit requires a strict and complete maintenance schedule. Remember that an hour's running time on a generator is equivalent to 42–82 miles on a vehicle engine. The need for frequent checks is obvious.

A great many generators are sold without engine hour meters. These register the time the engine has run. If the unit is not equipped with such a meter, you can buy one from an aftermarket dealer. The meter is relatively inexpensive and can be extremely helpful in keeping track of running hours and scheduled maintenance.

All generators come with an owner's manual which should be followed very closely for operating and maintenance instructions. Keep a close checklist of which maintenance procedures have been done and which have not.

The following general maintenance procedures should be carried out to ensure trouble-free operation.

Inspect the generator and its compartment housing every eight hours of running time. If dust or dirt has accumulated from off-road use, clean the unit with compressed air. Check the fuel supply and the oil level in the crankcase. Add to the reservoirs if they are below a safe level.

At the end of every 50 hours of running time, perform the eight-hour maintenance operation, service the air cleaner, and clean the governor linkage.

After 100 hours, perform the 50-hour operation, and clean and gap the spark plugs, change the oil, and clean out the crankcase breather.

As the running time increases on the generator, the maintenance schedule should be followed closely. If the generator runs for 200 hours, that is the equivalent of at least 8400 car miles. At the 200-hour interval, check all the components which were checked in the 100-hour examination and examine the ignition points, replacing them if they are badly worn, pitted, or burned. Clean the fuel filter and the top of the battery with water. If you operate your generator in warmer climates, check the battery more often. Remove the covering from the generator armature. Check and clean the connector ring at the point where the armature contacts the brushes. Replace the connector rings if they are worn to 5/16 in. or less. Replacement of any generator component is not an easy task. If you are not qualified to perform the maintenance procedures, take the unit to a qualified mechanic.

At 500 hours, the generator has run the equivalent of 21,000 car miles. The average generator runs at a relatively slow and constant speed, causing the combustion chambers to get coated with carbon deposits. It is wise to have the combustion chamber(s) cleaned and the valve clearance checked at this point.

For units which run at higher rpm, the maintenance schedule should be increased. To be certain, check the owner's manual for the correct settings, specifications, and frequency of the various maintenance operations.

Some generator manufacturers offer emergency parts kits containing component replacement parts for those common malfunctions which might occur while in the field. Such things as a point set, spark plugs, condenser, air cleaner, carburetor repair kits, fuel pump repair kits, choke element, and a selection of various gaskets are usually included in these kits. If the kits are not available, make up one of your own; it will be of great value if a breakdown occurs.

Generator Winterizing

If the generator is to be stored over the winter months, protective measures should be taken. All gasoline must be removed from the engine. This includes the tank, the lines, and the carburetor. If the gas is allowed to remain, it will turn gummy and clog the system. To remove all the gas, drain the tank and run the engine until it stops from a lack of fuel. This will drain the lines and the carburetor. Also remove the spark plug and squirt approximately one ounce of SAE 30 oil into the cylinder. Turn the engine over a few revolutions to distribute the oil and then replace the spark plug.

CHOOSING THE CORRECT SIZE GENERATOR

In order to determine the right size generator, add the total watts of all the appliances, lights, and equipment which are to be connected to the unit. Add the ratings which are usually located on the component name plate. For other equipment and power tools, check the horsepower rating and the type of motor.

The greatest generator drain is produced in starting the electrical components. Repulsion induction motors require two and one-half times the amount of current to start as it takes to maintain a running speed. Split-phase motors require as much as five times the running current. Universal motors, such as the type used in portable power tools and appliances, do not require extra starting current—only the running watts are figured.

To compute the number of watts required, if only the amps and volts are given, use the following formula:

Amps x Volts = Watts.

Use the following steps to determine the correct generator size.

1. Establish the total wattage of all appliances.

2. Analyze the motor loads and check for the starting wattage.

3. Determine which of the loads can be staggered for emergency use. In most cases, it is impractical to have an alternator that is large enough to handle the total connected load at one time.

Appliance and Equipment

Appliance	Watts	Equipment	Watts
Electric Iron	900	Hand Saw 8 in.	1500
TV Set	200–550	Electric Drill ½ in.	750
Toaster	1000	Electric Drill ¼ in.	250
Skillet	1250		
Coffee Maker	1000		
Radio	40–100		
Refrigerator	1200		
Electric Stove	3000–10,000		
Electric Water Heater	1000–5000		

Motor Starting Requirements
Approximate Starting Watts Required

Motor Rating (hp)	Approx Running Watts	Universal Motors	Repulsion Induction Motors	Capacitor Motors	Split Phase Motors
⅙	275	400	600	850	1200
¼	400	500	850	1050	1700
⅓	450	600	975	1350	1950
½	600	750	1300	1800	2600
¾	850	1000	1900	2600	✿
1	1000	1250	2300	3000	✿
1½	1600	✿	3200	4200	✿
2	2000	✿	3900	5100	✿
3	3000	✿	5200	6800	✿
5	4800	✿	7500	9800	✿

✿ Motors of higher horsepower shown in this classification are not generally used.

Alternator Capability for Electric Motor Starting

				Capacitor		Split Phase	
Alternator Rating In Watts	Universal	Repulsion Heavy Start Load	Induction Light Start Load	Heavy Start Load	Light Start Load	Heavy Start Load	Light Start Load
1000	½	—	—	—	—	—	—
1250	1	½	—	¼	—	¼	—
1750	1	½	¾	¼	½	⅓	—
2650	1½	1	1½	½	1	½	¾
3500	✿	2	2½	1½	2	✿	✿
5000	✿	2½	3	2	✿	✿	✿
7500	✿	4	5	2½	✿	✿	✿
1500	1	½	½	¼	¼	¼	✿
3000	2	1½	2	¾	1	¾	¾
5000	✿	2½	3	2½	3	✿	✿

TYPE OF MOTOR AND HP RATING

✿ Motors of higher horsepower rating than shown in this classification are not generally used.

LIST OF ELECTRICAL TERMS
FOR GENERATORS

ALTERNATOR—A device for generating alternating current using a revolving magnetic field (rotor) with power produced in stationary coils (stator).

AMPERE (Amp)—Unit of measure showing the rate of flow of current.

ALTERNATING CURRENT—Electrical current where the voltage changes from maximum positive to maximum negative in a given period of time. With 60 cycle current, this takes place 60 times per second.

BRUSHES—In an alternator, brushes carry a small amount of DC current to the revolving field (rotor) to maintain a strong magnetic field.

CIRCUIT—An electrical current requires a complete path in order to flow. This is called a circuit. Current will not flow through an open circuit, only a closed one.

CONDUCTOR—A substance or body that is capable of transmitting electricity.

CURRENT—The amount of electricity measured in amps which are flowing in a circuit.

CYCLE—A given length of time. (See alternating current.) In the U.S. most electric current is 60 cycles.

DIRECT CURRENT—A maintained flow of current at a steady voltage such as current from a battery. Different from an alternating current in that the alternating current moves from maximum positive to maximum negative in a given number of times per second (cycle).

DUAL VOLTAGE—A capability of offering both 115 V and 230 V simultaneously.

ELECTRICAL FORMULA—

    Kilowatt = 1000 watts
    Watts = volts x amps
    Amps = watts ÷ volts
    Volts = watts ÷ amps

EQUIPMENT GROUND—The frame or neutral side of the winding.

EXCITATION CURRENT—DC current required to maintain a magnetic field in the rotor.

FREQUENCY—Term designating the number of times per second an alternating current changes direction in a given period of time.

FIELD—In the creation of electricity, a magnetic field is necessary. In an alternator, the magnetic field turns with the rotor.

GROUND—Connection to the earth through a conductor for safety purposes.

KILOWATT—1000 watts.

OHM—Unit of measure of resistance.

OHM'S LAW—Voltage is equal to resistance of load x amps.

RECTIFIER—A device that changes AC current to DC current which is used to excite or maintain the field in the rotor of an alternator.

REACTOR—A device used to control the voltage and provide an instantaneous response from the generator when a load is applied and increased current is needed, or vice versa.

ROTOR—The revolving element of the alternator. It is the magnetic field.

SHORT—This describes the condition of an insulation breakdown between conductors.

VOLT (V)—The potential in an electrical circuit, similar to pressure in a water system.

VOLTAGE REGULATION—The amount of voltage change between no load and full load. A very important consideration in the starting of electric motors.

WATTS—A measure of total electrical energy.

WATT HOURS METER—A recording device to register kilowatt hours.

5 · Water and Sewage

The Water System

The water system in a chassis-mount or slide-in camper can vary from a water tank and a hand pump and drain to a fairly complicated plumbing system complete with water tank, electric pump with a pressure-sensitive switch, hot and cold water faucets, and all of the necessary drains which can empty either into a holding tank or out of the camper by way of a sewer line.

It is important that the owner of the vehicle become familiar with the trailer's

Pressurized water input

Non-pressurized water input

water supply to pressurize the system. The plumbing should be checked before connection to a pressurized outside line to make sure that the system will hold the pressure. (In most cities the water pressure ranges from 40 to 60 psi.) While most campers are able to cope with this pressure range, problems may arise with campground facilities where there is greater pressure. Therefore extra caution should be exercised in a campground.

Devices are available to reduce the pressure to a constant 35 psi. They are installed in the incoming line ahead of any other components. Some campers come with these units already installed.

The hand operated pump is installed in some slide-in units. It is mounted at the sink and works on the muscle principle: the harder you pump the more you get. The plunger in the cylinder of the pump creates a limited vacuum which moves the water from the water tank through the water line and out the faucet.

Electric pumps are fastened in an inline connection between the water tank and the faucets. The switch to activate the pump is sometimes located in the handle of the faucet. When the faucet is turned on, the circuit is closed and the pump starts to operate. When the water is turned off, so is the switch and the pump stops

water system layout. Refer to the owner's manual for a diagram of the system and to find the location of the major components.

THE WATER PUMP

There are a variety of water pumping systems installed in campers. Some of the units rely on the pressure from a city

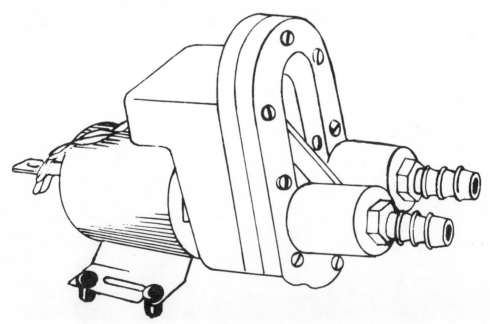

Water pump

Faucet assembly

running. This type of system is used on systems with only one faucet.

On campers with more than one faucet, it is rather inconvenient to install several electrical circuits to operate the pump, so a pressure-sensitive switch is installed in the output line of the pump. When the pressure decreases due to the opening of a faucet, the pump goes on; when the faucet is shut off, the pressure builds up and the switch turns off the pump.

One other system uses an air pump to induce pressure into the system. An electric motor is activated by a pressure-sensi-

Secondary basin

tive switch when the air pressure in the water tank is lowered to a certain point by the removal of water from the tank. The compressor forces air into the remaining air space in the tank. It is also possible to charge systems such as this with an air pressure hose found in gas stations. There is usually an air valve on the side of campers having this system so the system can be charged from the outside. It is also possible to pressurize the tank by using a hand tire pump. In fact it is a good idea to carry such a unit just in case the compressor fails.

NOTE: *Remember to turn off the main switch to the water pump when the pump is not being used.*

A fuse should be installed in the power line to the water pump as close to the power source as possible. A filter should be in the line from the water source to the pump to prevent any harmful sand or grit from damaging the mechanism.

Water Pump Removal

Use the following procedure to remove the water pump from the camper.

1. Turn off the water supply at the tank and then the pump switch.

2. Remove the electrical connections to the pump.

3. Remove the input and output hoses to the pump, making certain to tag each for reassembly.

4. Remove the pump attaching screws and remove the pump from the camper.

5. To install the unit, reverse the above procedure.

Water Pump Troubleshooting Chart

Condition	Remedy
Pump runs but there is no pressure	1. Check the water level in the holding tank. 2. Make certain that the electrical power is sufficient. 3. See that all the required valves are open. 4. Check for leaks. 5. Check for suction at the pump. If there is none, the pump must be repaired or replaced.
Noise in the pump	1. Examine the pump mounting bolts for looseness. 2. Make certain that both inlet and outlet hoses are clear and properly installed. 3. If the faucet has an aerator, remove it and check for blockage.
Pump does not run	1. Check the electrical connections for contact. 2. Check the amount of current to the pump motor. 3. Examine the pump for defects.

Priming the System

1. Fill the fresh water holding tank, making sure all the drain valves are closed.

2. Energize the main current to the pump.

3. Keep all outlets open until water appears.

4. Close the outlet and de-energize the pump (if the pump is equipped with a manual energizer switch.)

NOTE: *Large amounts of iron and lime deposits are found in the water of some sections of the country. Because of this, it is a good idea to flush the water tank frequently by mixing a cleaning solution of bicarbonate of soda and water (1/4–1/2 lbs of soda). This mixture is then poured into the water tank and left overnight. Rinse the tank clean and refill it with drinking water.*

WATER HEATER

Water heaters are not always included in smaller slide-in models, but on the larger units they are usually available at least as an option. The heater is one more means of bringing the comforts of home with you when you are away from home.

Water heater

Water heater external exhaust vent with water intake port

There are basically two types of water heaters: gas and electric. The gas type heats the water by means of a flame encompassing the cold water coils while the electric type heats the water by transferring heat from the electric coils which surround the water jackets. Neither type will work correctly with any air in its water system. Allow water to run from all the hot water faucets until it flows smoothly.

Gas operated heaters work on the same principle as gas operated refrigerators

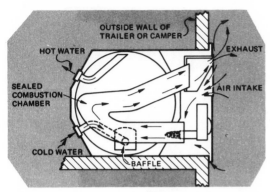

Internal workings of a water heater

(see "Refrigerator"). They utilize a thermocouple. The same procedure is used to start the pilot on the heater as is used to start the pilot on the refrigerator.

Since the heater's operating principles are similar to those of the gas operated refrigerator, it can have approximately the same malfunctions. If the heater does not operate, check the obvious causes first. It is usually something simple such as having the LP gas run out or the pilot blow out. Malfunctions in the electric system are few but the ones that usually occur are shorted or loose wires caused by vibration.

Lighting the Pilot

If the pilot has blown out, it is a good idea to open the pilot door and allow the unit to air for approximately 15 minutes with the selector lever turned off so that any trapped gas can escape. Once this is done use the following procedure.

1. Rotate the selector to the "pilot" position.

2. Depress the pilot button. In some

The main burner Primary and Secondary combustion air is taken from outside the coach, and reaches the burner through the built in base openings. No air adjustments are provided, or necessary for the main burner.

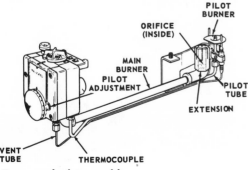

Burner and pilot assembly

cases it is necessary to depress the selector button.

3. Light the pilot either by using a match or one of the built in lighting assemblies offered on new units.

4. After the pilot is lit, keep the button depressed for one minute to allow the thermocouple to heat. Then release the button; the pilot should remain lit.

Pilot Adjustment

On new models there are no facilities for adjusting the pilots. As long as the correct pressure is supplied to the unit and the orifices are clean, the pilot should work properly.

Older units have an air adjustment which can be regulated. Before any adjustment is made, make certain that the LP gas system is delivering the correct pressure to the unit. It should be 11 in. of water column.

Adjust the air for the pilot to obtain a blue flame. There is too much air if the pilot flame is lifting from the burner. Lack of air will cause a yellow flame and a sooty condition.

NOTE: *It is important that the flue pipes are installed properly and free of blockage.*

In some cases an off-colored flame is caused by an obstruction in the air supply tube located just before the burner. This blockage may be removed by forcing compressed air through the line.

Storage

Whenever the unit is stored, especially during the winter when the temperature is below freezing, it is necessary to drain the water heater. This procedure is done in conjunction with draining the entire water system. Open the drain valve of the water heater and allow the unit to drain completely. (See "Storage and Winterizing.")

The Sewage System

Most camper units, in order to become more self sufficient, include some type of sewage system. Although the systems vary, most include plumbing and some type of holding tank assembly with drain valves for dumping.

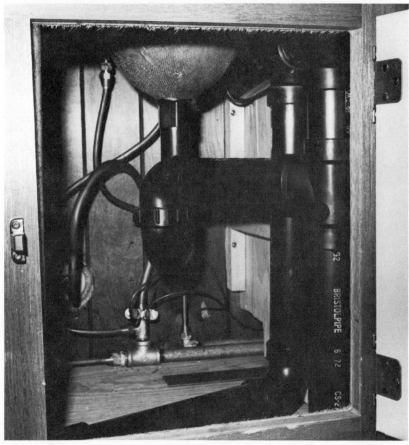

Camper plumbing

Most campers which have holding tanks use the single tank design but some use two tanks which separate waste from the wash basin and sink from toilet waste.

It is wise to consult the owner's manual for the location and routing of the plumbing lines and the recommended chemicals to be installed into the holding tank. These chemicals are added to deodorize and dissolve waste matter in the tank. NOTE: *If the Thermasan* ® *Waste Destruction System is used in the camper, the special chemicals recommended by the manufacturer must be used.*

TYPES OF TOILET ASSEMBLIES

There are three types of toilets used in the campers. They are the fresh water type, the recirculating type, and the portable type.

The fresh water type works, as the name indicates, from the fresh water holding tank. Each time the unit is used, the pump circulates a new supply of water through the toilet and transfers it with the waste to the holding tank.

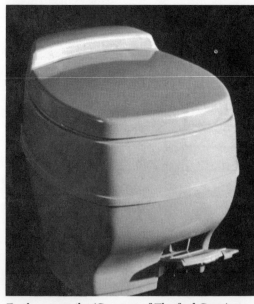

Fresh water toilet (Courtesy of Thetford Corp.)

Recirculating type toilet (Courtesy of Thetford Corp.)

Toilet assembly with shower

Portable type toilet (Courtesy of Thetford Corp.)

The recirculating type toilet was adapted from aircraft use. It is a completely independent unit powered by an electric motor. There is a storage facility for approximately eight gallons of fluid inside the tank. The system is "charged" with four gallons of clean water and the recommended chemicals, and is good for about 80 to 100 usages. On campers equipped with holding tanks, the toilet may be drained into the tank and the unit may be recharged.

Portable type toilets are most common on the slide-in units. These are most popular because of their portability, size, and relatively small amount of maintenance. The unit is totally self-contained and con-

sists of a toilet assembly and two separate tanks. One tank holds fresh water while the other acts as the holding tank. The chemicals are added to the holding tank.

There are usually two foot controls: one lever to open the holding tank valve to allow the entrance of the waste from the bowl to the holding tank, and the pump lever which will circulate the fresh water from the fresh water tank into the toilet bowl. Most of the units include a detachable waste tank which can be removed for disposal.

Toilet Installation

Before you start cutting holes in the floor of your camper the idea of installing a toilet in a unit which has none should be examined closely. Do you have the space to spare? Will you have to install a holding tank? Will the unit accommodate a holding tank? Where will you put it? And just what type do you want? All of these questions must be examined along with the size of the family and many other variables, before the final decision is made. It is a wise idea to consult a reputable dealer before making such a decision.

Once you decide which type of unit you want the next problem is where to put it. It is hard to give up valuable storage space, but if a good job of installation is done there might not be too much space lost. Since the location of the holding tank is usually below the unit it is necessary to position the unit where the structural design of the camper will accommodate it. The final decision for both placement and installation lies with your dealer. It is recommended that he perform the operation on your camper. He has both the facilities and the knowledge to make the installation a simple task.

SHOWER ASSEMBLY

Showers are offered as options in some of the more expensive campers. They consist of pump fed shower heads on flexible cords. Until recently, this luxury was available only in travel trailers.

Bath areas have plastic or simulated tile floors with central drains which are connected into separate or universal holding

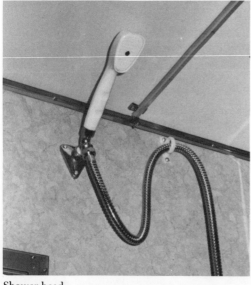

Shower head

tanks. By closing the cover on the toilet, the entire bath area can be converted into a shower.

Routine Maintenance

The sewage system should be cleaned thoroughly after every trip so that it is free of blockage.

If the unit is used when the temperature drops below freezing, add antifreeze solution to the charge. Check the manufacturer's literature for the recommended type.

EMPTYING THE SYSTEM

If the camper is equipped with a holding tank, a direct line can be connected from the toilet to the holding tank to allow the toilet to be drained at will.

If there is no holding tank available, connect a hose to the drainage duct at the base of the toilet assembly, and slowly open the discharge valve to release the waste. Discharge the waste only at a proper disposal station. Once the waste is discharged, fill the unit with 4 to 6 gallons of water and ½ cup of toilet cleaner. Leave the mixture overnight for the best results, then drain and flush the unit with clean water before recharging.

Winterizing the System

Drain the input line to the toilet assembly and then, by pumping the foot pedal of the toilet, remove all the water from the system. It is important to remove *all* water since freezing temperatures will cause water expansion and damage to the plumbing system.

The holding tank should be cleaned, rinsed, and drained of all water and then if possible blown dry with compressed air. Once the system is drained, check with your dealer for special winterizing concentrates to be added to the holding tank to prevent rust, corrosion and other harmful effects of low temperature. The owner's manual may also have recommendations for a cold weather protective charge.

If the camper is to be used during the winter season, the system must be protected from freezing. There are a great number of commercial antifreeze additives which can be used, but first consult your dealer for his recommendations.

WATER TANK REMOVAL

Because of the variety of water tank locations in slide-in and chassis-mount units, the procedure listed below is a general removal procedure which can be adapted for any model.

1. Drain the water tank completely.
2. Remove the connections from the inlet, outlet, and vent hoses.
3. Make sure all connections to the tank are removed (including electrical connections).
4. Remove any tank shielding.
5. Remove the tank supports while bracing the tank assembly from the bottom.
6. Remove the tank from the chassis.
7. Installation may be accomplished by reversing the removal procedure.

NOTE: *Any insulating material which is removed must be replaced when the tank is reinstalled.*

THE HOLDING TANK

Holding tanks used on chassis-mount and slide-in camper units vary in size from 15–25 gallons in capacity.

Generally there are three types of drainage systems: single tank; two tank; and the by-pass holding tank systems.

In a single tank system all the drainage outlets (sink, basin, toilet) empty into one holding tank. This necessitates a larger holding tank than the other systems. The two tank system provides one tank which is directly connected to the toilet and another tank which holds the waste from the sink, basin and shower (if applicable). The by-pass system uses a holding tank for toilet waste while all other waste from the camper is channeled from the camper, either through a sewer line or a catch receptacle.

Emptying the Holding Tank

NOTE: *It is extremely important that the holding tank of any camper be emptied only at an approved disposal site.*

The tank can be drained by fastening the discharge hose from the camper to the fitting on the sewer opening. Make certain that both connections, at the camper and at the sewer, are secure as there will be a fair amount of pressure flowing through the waste line. Once the tank is empty it should be cleaned with fresh water. It is important to wash out the inside of the drain hose also. Finally, insert the recommended chemicals and the system will be ready for use.

Thermasan®

The Thermasan Waste Destruction System is a relatively new addition to the recreational vehicle appliance market. This system uses the ultra high temperature of the vehicle exhaust to completely burn the waste stored in the holding tank. Since the exhaust system sometimes reaches temperatures of 900 to 1000° F total destruction is possible.

The greatest advantage of the system is that the hold tank needs to be emptied less frequently. It does not completely do away with having to find a dumping station, since the system is not functioning constantly. The Thermasan System will not operate at speeds lower than 30 mph.

The system itself is broken down into two sub-systems, the plumbing circuit and the electrical circuits. Most of the plumbing hardware is mounted in the camper while the sending units for the electrical circuits are mounted in the truck.

The following is a list of the components in the system. They are divided into plumbing and electrical assemblies.

PLUMBING

1. The evacuation probe in the holding tank.
2. The rubber tubing which runs to the quick disconnect on slide-in camper models.
3. A metering injection assembly that regulates the flow of waste material into the truck's exhaust system.
4. The liquid quick-disconnect coupler which is used in slide-in camper models.
5. The Sanijector, which is hooked into the truck's exhaust system. The Sanijector's nozzle sprays the treated waste into the exhaust pipes.

Also included in the plumbing components are the chemicals that are placed in the holding tank to break down and deodorize the waste material.

ELECTRICAL

1. A level sensor that signals when the holding tank is empty so that the system will shut off.
2. Electrical quick disconnects which are positioned between the camper and the truck on slide-in units.

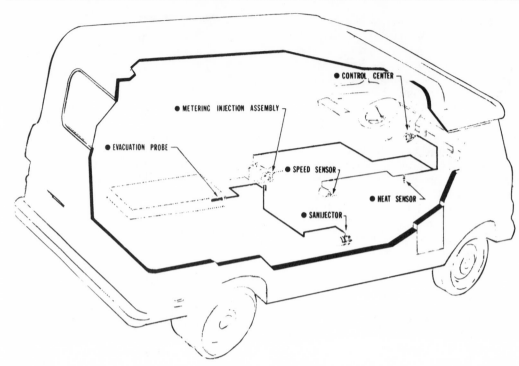

Chassis-mount schematic

3. The speed sensor that signals the unit when the truck is traveling at a sufficient speed to cause the system to operate.

4. A heat sensor that signals the unit when the exhaust gases are hot enough to burn the treated waste.

5. The control box, which is mounted under the truck dash panel. This control

Metering injection assembly (Courtesy of Thermasan Corp.)

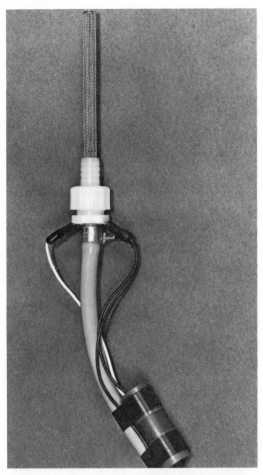

Evacuation probe (Courtesy of Thermasan Corp.)

The Sanijector (Courtesy of Thermasan Corp.)

unit monitors vehicle speed and exhaust system temperature. If either the speed or the temperature of exhaust drops below certain levels, the unit stops pumping the treated waste into the exhaust system.

On the control panel there are three lights positioned across the front of the unit. One of the lights indicates whether

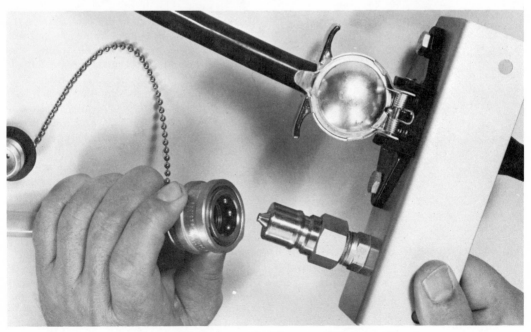

Liquid quick disconnect coupler (Courtesy of Thermasan Corp.)

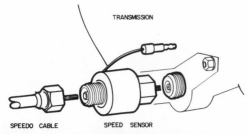

Speed sensor (Courtesy of Thermasan Corp.)

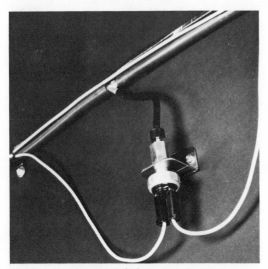

Heat sensor (Courtesy of Thermasan Corp.)

Control panel (Courtesy of Thermasan Corp.)

switch has been put in the ON position.

Let us assume that you have already put the chemical solvent in the holding tank and the system is ready for use. You are on the road driving at about 50 mph and are expecting to maintain that speed for some time.

Once the unit is switched on, the red light will come on at the control panel. The heat sensor signals the control center whether or not the exhaust system is hot enough to burn the waste. If so, then the control center closes an electrical circuit to the speed sensor. The speed sensor tells whether or not the car is traveling fast enough. If it is, an electrical circuit is closed to the control center. When the circuit is closed, a green light comes on and the control center closes another electrical circuit to the metering injection assembly. The metering assembly begins to drain the holding tank through the evacuation probe. The waste material flows up to the metering injection assembly and from there is regulated and pumped through the quick-disconnect coupler to the Sanijector. The treated waste is injected into the exhaust pipe and completely destroyed. All wastes, bacteria, and gaseous by-products are destroyed and rendered odorless and harmless. When the tank is almost empty, a white light comes on at the control panel indicating that you should soon turn off the system. The light is activated by the level sensor in the holding tank. When the tank is empty, the green light goes out telling the operator that the pump has stopped and the unit must be turned off.

There are three types of Thermasan arrangements for chassis-mount and slide-in units. One unit is for holding tanks that collect both toilet wastes and sink, basin, and shower wastes. Another type is only used to evacuate toilet wastes. The third type of unit is for campers with two holding tanks: one for toilet wastes only, and one for sink, basin, and wash water waste. The Thermasan unit for this system draws from both tanks at the same rate.

Odors

If odors should develop don't immediately conclude that the system is malfunctioning; it may be temporarily insufficient exhaust system heat. This can happen during a heavy rain storm when

the unit is on while the other two tell if the unit is burning the treated waste and if the holding tank is empty. There is also an ON/OFF switch located on the control panel face.

The following is an explanation of how the system works after the ON/OFF

water is splashing on the exhaust pipes and cooling them.

NOTE: *Frequently check the quick disconnect couplers on slide-in units to make sure they are clean and sealing correctly.*

Installation

The installation of the Thermasan is a fairly complicated procedure. Unless you have a reasonable amount of mechanical ability, have the unit installed by a qualified dealer.

If you order the unit, the kit should include:

1. A hardware package
2. The wiring harness assembly
3. Metering injection assembly
4. PCV hose
5. The tank sensor assembly
6. Evacuation probe assembly
7. Level indicator (optional)

The above items are installed in the camper portion of the unit while the following items are installed on the truck.

1. Control center assembly
2. Speed sensor assembly
3. Heat sensor assembly
4. Sanijector assembly
5. Quick-disconnect assembly
6. Harness assembly
7. Silicone hose
8. Hardware package

MOUNTING THE CONTROL CENTER MODULE TO THE DASH OF THE VEHICLE

Position the control center module where it is visible to the vehicle operator but not where it will obstruct vision.

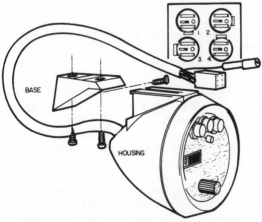

Mounted Control Module (Courtesy of Thermasan Corp.)

The unit is attached by:

1. Drilling ⅛ in. diameter holes in the dash and then attaching the base of the control box to the dash with no. 6 screws ½ in. long.

2. The control slides onto the base and snaps securely in place.

3. Also insert a ½ in. no. 6 screw into the side of the control box to insure a stable mounting of the panel.

INSTALLATION OF THE HEAT SENSOR UNIT

The heat sensor unit is, in effect, a vacuum-sensing unit. Since there is a direct relationship between vacuum condition in the intake manifold and the amount of heat that is expelled into the exhaust pipes of the vehicle, the heat sensor can be installed in any vacuum line that is directly connected to the intake manifold. Make certain, however, that there is a strong, constant vacuum in the line when the engine is running at an idle speed.

If the hose to the heat sensor has to be shortened it must be done at the engine side of the hose as an in-line restrictor is at the other end.

4. To mount the heat sensor, drill ⁹⁄₆₄ in. diameter holes into the firewall at the desired position and mount the unit with two no. 8 screws ¾ in. long.

5. Cut the crankcase ventilation hose and insert the "T" fitting provided with the hose or the larger one in the hardware package. No clamps are necessary.

INSTALLATION OF THE SPEED SENSOR TO THE TRANSMISSION

Since there are various manufacturers of truck transmissions, Thermasan provides a variety of adaptors to mount the speed sensor to most American transmissions. There is also a separate set of directions enclosed in the adaptor package to simplify selection of the correct adaptor.

6. Once the correct adaptor has been selected, remove the speedometer cable at the transmission.

7. Attach the speed sensor to the transmission. Screw the sensor ¼ turn past finger-tight. Do not overtighten.

8. Replace the speedometer cable to the speed sensor, screwing it ¼ turn past finger-tight. Do not overtighten.

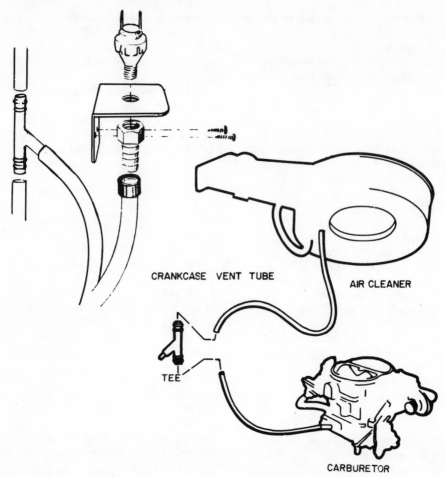

Installation of heat sensor (Courtesy of Thermasan Corp.)

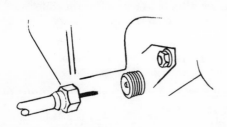

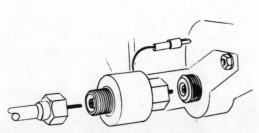

Speed sensor adaptor (Courtesy of Thermasan Corp.)

INSTALLATION OF THE SANIJECTOR

To install this unit it is necessary to drill a ½ in. hole in the exhaust pipe of the vehicle. This hole should be drilled as close to the exhaust manifolds as possible. It should be ahead of the muffler but behind any catalytic pollution control devices. It is necessary, when installing the Sanijector, to set the screen end of the unit into the hole.

NOTE: *The hose from the unit must be at least 2 inches from the exhaust pipes at all places.*

Install the clamps and tighten the unit in place. The gasket will tighten sufficiently to make a seal.

INSTALLATION OF THE TANK EVACUATION PROBE

The evacuation probe must be installed a few inches above the bottom of the hold-

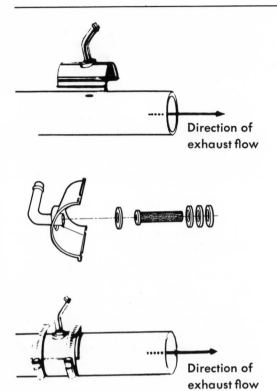

Sanijector installation (Courtesy of Thermasan Corp.)

NOTE: *If inserting the probe is difficult, use soap as a lubricant.*

To install the metering injection assembly, bolt the unit to the chassis using $\frac{3}{8}$ x 1 in. bolts.

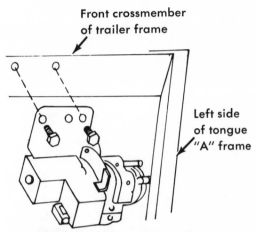

Installation of the metering injection assembly (Courtesy of Thermasan Corp.)

ing tank. This allows solids to break up and toilet paper to separate through chemical agitation. Failure to mount the probe above the bottom of the tank will result in clogging of the probe. This would mean that the Thermasan would not be capable of fully emptying the holding tank. The probe should not be installed near the dump valve outlet.

Use the following procedure to install the unit.

1. Using a hole saw, cut a $\frac{3}{4}$ in. hole in the holding tank and insert the grommet supplied for this purpose.

2. Insert the tank probe into the grommet.

INSTALLATION OF HOSES

1. The silicone rubber hose is connected to the Sanijector. Cut it to the proper length and connect the other end to the pump outlet.

2. The grey plastic hose should be cut to the proper length and attached from the pump inlet to the tank evacuation probe.

NOTE: *The grey waste lines are to be used between the holding tank and the pump. The milk colored waste line is for connection between the Sanijector and the pump.*

CAUTION: *Because of the extreme pressure the milky hose must withstand, no other hose can be substituted.*

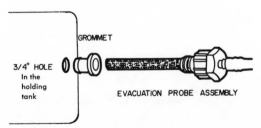

Installation of the evacuation probe (Courtesy of Thermasan Corp.)

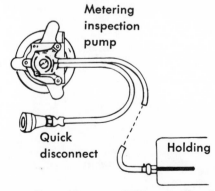

Hose installation (Courtesy of Thermasan Corp.)

3. Route the hoses underneath the vehicle and secure them. Make sure that they are clear of any hot or abrasive areas.

Installing the Level Indicator Module

CAUTION: *It is of extreme importance that all power to the system is off before installing the level indicator.*

1. After installing the evacuation probe, make sure that the two screws in the probe are at a 45° angle with the yellow lead on top.

CAUTION: *When installing the clamp on the hose of the evacuation probe, do not touch the screws or terminals.*

2. Install the black and yellow wires onto either of the terminals on the evacuation probe.

3. The plug for the module can be inserted into its counterpart in the harness. Connect the module to the evacuation probe hose using either electrical tape or tie wraps. Do not pinch the hose.

NOTE: *When installing the wiring harness, wait until the hoses are in place because you may wish to route and fasten them together.*

Checking the Unit

1. Turn the Thermasan control center switch to the ON position.

   a. The green light should come on unless the unit is wired to the ignition.

   b. The white light will come on if the holding tank is empty.

   c. The red light should not come on.

2. Remove that wire from the terminal on the heat sensor which connects the heat sensor to the speed sensor.

3. Ground the heat sensor to the terminal. The red light will appear and the pump will run.

4. Start the engine and increase the rpm to slightly higher than idle. The red light will go out and the pump will stop. Allow at least fifteen seconds for the light to go out.

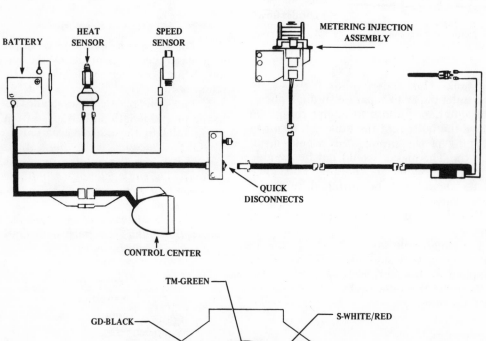

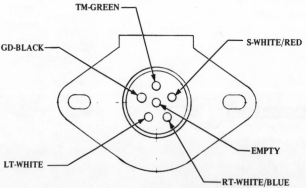

Wiring diagram (Courtesy of Thermasan Corp.)

NOTE: *On slide-in units the white light will remain lit when the camper is removed.*

ROAD CHECK (WITH THE THERMASAN CONTROL SWITCHED ON)

1. Accelerate to 45 mph. The red light on the control panel will come on between 25 and 35 mph.
2. Remove your foot from the accelerator. The red light will go out in 2–6 seconds.
3. Accelerate again to 45 mph. The red light will come on in 2–6 seconds.
4. Remove your foot from the accelerator and the red light should go out.
5. Drive the vehicle on a relatively flat highway at 45 mph for ½ mile. The red light will stay on until deceleration.
6. Press the "press to test" button on the control center when the red light is lit. If the red and green lights flash on and off together this shows that the unit is pumping the waste.
NOTE: *The white light will appear when the level in the holding tank is nearing the bottom.*

Troubleshooting Guide

This Thermasan troubleshooting guide is designed to give fast and easy solutions to service problems. To use the guide, simply select the particular symptoms observed and match them with the "Problem Index" below. The sequence of steps for locating the cause of the particular problems have been carefully designed to save time. Skipping steps will not save time but will make locating the problem more difficult if not impossible. After replacing a part, recheck the system. Test drive the unit to be sure that everything is operating properly.

PROBLEM INDEX

Problems

1. Neither the ready nor the reaction light glows when the system is turned on.
2. The ready light works but there is no reaction light.
3. The reaction light works but there is no ready light.
4. Both lights work but the unit does not seem to pump waste.
5. The reaction light stays on even when decelerating.
6. Both ready and reaction lights are flickering on and off.
7. The ready light flickers on and off.
8. The reaction light flickers on and off.
9. Both ready and reaction lights operate but do not pulse when the press-to-test button is pushed.
10. The empty light does not come on.
11. The empty light does not go off.

Odor Problems

1. Odors are noticeable inside the vehicle while driving.
2. Odors are noticeable outside the vehicle after operating the Thermasan.
3. Residual odors at the tailpipe.

Problem

1. Neither the ready nor the reaction lights appear when the system is turned on.

Remedy

a. Inspect the connection at the battery for possible corrosion or loose connections. If the terminals are corroded, clean them with fine sandpaper and return the *red* lead to the positive (+) terminal and the *black* lead to the negative (−) terminal. Tighten all connections.
b. Remove and inspect the in-line fuse on the red lead near the battery connection. If the fuse has blown this is evidence of a short in the electrical system. The entire harness and its connections should be inspected for frayed or burned wires or loose connections.
WARNING: *Do not replace the 5 amp fuse until the harness has been inspected. Under no circumstances should a higher amp rated fuse be used.*
c. Check the connector between the harness and the control center module for proper connections. The male and female pins housed within the connector body should be straight and of equal height, and firmly attached to their respective wires. Compare the number of holes at the rear of the connector and the color of the wire inserted in that hole with the diagram provided. When the inspection is completed, carefully mate the connector bodies and press firmly until the snap tabs are locked into place.
d. Test the switch and its connections for defects. Remove the setscrew from the

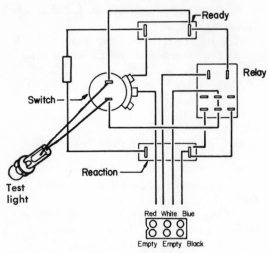

Testing the switch (Courtesy of Thermasan Corp.)

side of the base on the control center module. Slide the control center off its base by exerting a firm forward pull. Remove the screw from the back of the control center and separate the housing from the bezel. Using a test light for locating shorts, check the switch. Reinstall the control center module.

Problem

2. The ready light works, but there is no reaction light after 35 mph.

Remedy

a. Check the reaction light for a burned out bulb and/or loose connections. Remove the setscrew from the side of the base on the control center module. Slide

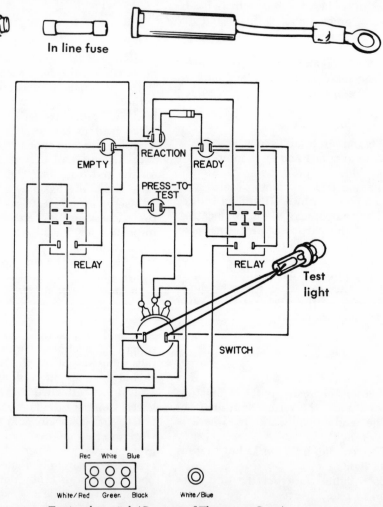

Testing the switch (Courtesy of Thermasan Corp.)

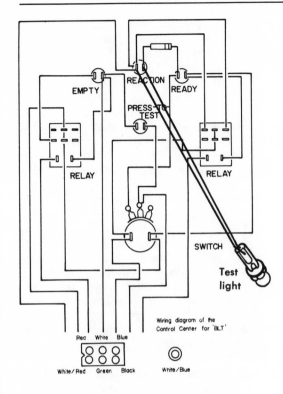

Wiring diagram of the
Control Center for 'BLT'

Red   White   Blue

White/Red   Green   Black   White/Blue

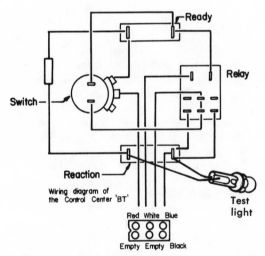

Wiring diagram of
the Control Center 'BT'

Red White Blue

Empty Empty Black

Testing the reaction light for a burned out bulb
(Courtesy of Thermasan Corp.)

proper connections. The male and female pins housed within the connector body should be straight and of equal height. They should be firmly attached to their respective wires. Compare the number of holes at the rear of the connector, and the color of the wire inserted in that hose with the diagram provided. When the inspection is completed, carefully mate the connector bodies and press firmly until the snap tabs are locked firmly into place.

c. Check the heat sensor leads for loose connections at the terminals.

d. To test for a faulty relay, remove the blue lead which travels from the harness to the heat sensor. With the system turned on, ground the lead to any clean unpainted portion of the frame. If the ready light does not appear, the relay is faulty. Replace the control center module. See "Installation Instructions" for more details.

e. Test for a faulty heat sensor. With the system turned on but the engine not running, ground the blue lead from the heat sensor to the speed sensor. If the system does not operate, the heat sensor is at fault. Remove the terminals and hose from the heat sensor. Remove the heat sensor from the vehicle by extracting the two screws from the bracket. Replace by reversing this procedure.

f. If, after testing for the above, the system does not operate at 35 mph the problem lies with the speed sensor and it must be replaced. Remove the speedometer cable from the speed sensor and disconnect its electrical fitting. Unscrew the speed sensor and replace it.

Problem

3. The reaction light works, but there is no ready light.

Remedy

a. Check the ready light for a burned out bulb and/or loose connections. Remove the setscrew from the side of the base on the control center module. Slide the control center off its base by pulling forward. Remove the screw from the back of the control center and separate the housing from the bezel. Using a test light check the ready light for a burned out bulb. Inspect the connections and reinstall the unit.

the control center off its base by exerting a firm forward pull. Remove the screw from the back of the control center and separate the housing from the bezel. Using a test light, test the reaction light for a burned out bulb. Inspect all connections and reinstall by reversing the above steps.

b. Inspect the connector between the harness and the control center module for

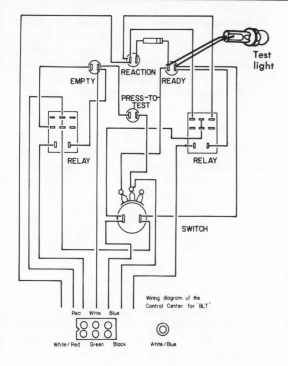

Wiring diagram of the Control Center for 'BLT'

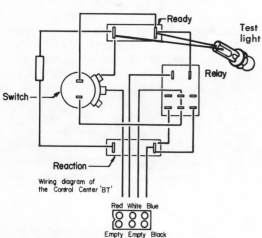

Wiring diagram of the Control Center 'BT'

Testing the ready light for a burned out bulb (Courtesy of Thermasan Corp.)

Problem

4. Both lights work, but the unit does not seem to pump waste.

Remedy

a. Examine the pump motor leads for good connection. Remove the two pan head screws which hold the terminal dust cover in place. Check the terminals and their leads for faulty connection. Also inspect the connections in the plastic pin housing that plugs into the dust cover. Re-

turn it to position and replace the screws.

b. Inspect all waste lines for possible kinks. Manually straighten any kinks and secure the hoses.

c. The waste lines or the hose menders within those lines may be plugged. Remove the blue wire from the harness side of the heat sensor and short that lead to the vehicle body. With the system turned on, watch the metering injection pump hoses for movement of waste. If waste does not move, go directly to step e. for solutions. If no waste is moving at this point, drain the contents of the holding tank. If the hose on the inlet side of the pump has collapsed, the plug should be found in the hose mender at the pump, the grey waste hose, or at the evacuation probe. (The evacuation probe plug is covered under step d.) Remove the grey hose at the hose mender near the pump. Operate the system again, as above. If the inlet hose to the pump collapses, the blockage is in the hose mender and can be cleaned with a steel rod. If the hose does not collapse with the grey line disconnected, the blockage is within the grey line or the evacuation probe. The grey line can be cleaned with compressed air or a steel rod. If, after cleaning the line and returning the hose to position, the pump still does not pump waste, the evacuation probe has become plugged. Check step d. for instructions.

NOTE: *In some rare instances, a blockage may occur in the hose mender on the outlet side of the pump causing a ballooning of that hose and a subsequent rupture of that line at the pump. In this case the hose within the pump must be replaced.*

To remove the pump, extract the two $5/16$ in. nuts from the thumbscrews which hold the front of the pump in place. Pull the front from the pump and remove the old hose from the rollers. Depress the springs on the hose menders and hold them in position. Slide the hose into position on the rollers and replace the front of the pump.

CAUTION: *Make sure the two halves of the pump assembly are not pinching the hose.*

Replace the two thumbscrews, tightening the nuts until the lockwashers flatten. Do not overtighten. Insert the tabs on the springs into the holes in the pump. Reclamp the waste lines to the inlet and outlet hose menders.

REMINDER: *The pump shaft rotates counter-clockwise. The grey waste line has to be attached to the inlet side.*

d. Remove the holding tank evacuation probe and inspect it for a possible clog. Remove the evacuation probe screen by unscrewing the plastic nut on the outside of the holding tank. If your system contains a level control, remove the terminals first and then note the alignment of the terminal screws. After separating the nut, remove the rubber washer and draw out the screen. Flush the screen to remove the plug. Insert the screen and press the rubber washer back into place. Screw the nut back into its fitting. If your system has the level indicator, orient the two terminal screws as before and plug the terminal wires back into place.

NOTE: *Either lead can be placed on the right or left terminal.*

e. Inspect the clamps on the grey waste line. Loose clamps will allow air to be pumped through the system instead of waste. Make certain that all clamps are tight.

f. Press the evacuation probe more firmly into the rubber grommet. Here, too, an air leak may occur and not allow the full potential to be drawn from the holding tank.

g. Inspect the hose to the Sanijector for possible burning. The burning of this hose is usually accompanied by an odor problem and is caused by an air leak between the metering injection assembly and the Sanijector. The hose must be replaced with the same high-temperature hose and the air leak prevented by tightening the clamps sufficiently.

CAUTION: *Do not substitute any other hose.*

If the Thermasan is installed on a slide-in camper unit, the quick disconnect should be examined for leakage. Replace if necessary.

Problem

5. The reaction light stays on even when decelerating.

Remedy

a. In this case the heat sensor is defective and should be replaced. To test for a faulty heat sensor, turn on the system with the engine not running and ground the blue lead which runs from the heat sensor

to the speed sensor. If the system does not operate, the heat sensor is at fault and must be replaced. Remove the mounting bracket and the heat sensor by removing the two screws from the bracket and pulling the hose from the hose barb fitting. Reinstall by reversing the above procedure.

Problem

6. Both the ready and reaction lights flicker on and off.

Remedy

a. If the lights are flickering on and off at a constant rate, the problem stems from the press-to-test feature. Remove the set-screw from the side of the base on the control center module. Slide the control center off its base by pulling forward. Remove the screw from the back of the control center housing and separate the housing from the bezel. Using a test lamp for locating shorts, check the press-to-test button. Also inspect the leads for broken solder joints. If the press-to-test is at fault, replace the control center module. See "Installation Instructions" for details.

b. If the ground to the battery is not

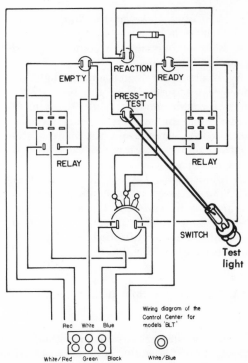

Checking the press-to-test button (Courtesy of Thermasan Corp.)

connected, the ready and reaction lights may flicker at a constant rate. Inspect the contact of the black wire at the battery. Clean the terminal and tighten in place.

c. If the lights flicker intermittently, the red line from the battery or the fuse block should be checked over its entire length. In addition, inspect the connection at the plastic connector near the control center and the connections at the ON/OFF switch in the control center. Begin by inspecting the red lead for possible frayed spots or bare areas. Inspect the six pin plastic connector for bent pins or loose connections at the pins. Remove the control center module by removing the setscrew from the side of the base. Slide the control center off the base by pulling forward. Remove the screw from the back of the control center housing and separate it from the bezel. Inspect the switch for broken solder joints. Replace by reversing the above instructions. If the problem still exists, a new control center must be installed. See "Installation Instructions" for details.

Problem

7. The green light flickers on and off.

Remedy

a. A lead is loose at the light, at the ON/OFF switch, at the battery or at the fuse block. Make sure all connections are secure and not corroded.

b. To check the switch and the light, remove the setscrew from the base of the control center module. Slide the control center from the base by pulling forward. Remove the screw from the back of the control center housing and separate it from the bezel. Check the switch for broken solder joints. Inspect the terminals at the light for loose contacts and reassemble the module by reversing the above procedure. If the problem still exists, a new control center must be installed. See "Installation Instructions" for details.

Problem

8. The reaction light flickers on and off.

Remedy

a. If the flicker is constant, then the speed sensor is faulty and must be replaced. Using a wrench, remove the speedometer cable from the speed switch. Disconnect the electrical supply to the speed sensor. Remove the speed sensor from the transmission. Reinstall the replacement parts by reversing the above procedure. CAUTION: *When tightening the speed sensor to the transmission, one quarter turn past finger tight is sufficient. Do not overtighten.*

b. If the flicker is intermittent, a connection is loose. Beginning at the connection with the battery or fuse block, inspect all terminals and connections. Inspect the blue wire to the heat sensor and speed sensor for a possible short or incomplete connection. Disconnect the six pin plastic connector near the control center module and inspect the pins to be certain that they are seated properly and making a good connection. Carefully mate the connector bodies again and press firmly so that they lock together. If the problem still exists, a new control center must be installed. See "Installation Instructions" for details.

Problem

9. Both the ready and reaction lights operate but do not pulse when the press-to-test button is pressed.

Remedy

a. Check the one pin connector near the control center module. Inspect the pin and socket for a loose connection. Mate the plastic housings until the snap connector catches.

b. Inspect the connection of the blue/white wire at the pump. Remove the two screws from the terminal duct cover on the motor. Check the blue/white wire for a broken solder joint or poor connection with its terminal. Replace the terminal cover and screws.

c. Remove the control center and inspect the press-to-test switch for broken solder joints. Remove the setscrew from the side of the control center base. Pull forward on the housing to separate it from the base. Remove the screw from the back of the housing to separate the bezel from the housing. Inspect the press-to-test switch for broken leads. Using a test lamp for locating shorts, test for a faulty press-to-test switch. If the switch is faulty, replace the control center assembly. See "Installation Instructions" for details.

Problem

10. The empty light does not come on. NOTE: *This may simply indicate that the holding tank level is not low enough to trigger the light. If the holding tank has been drained and the light does not come on, begin your investigation at the evacuation probe.*

Remedy

a. Visually inspect the clamp which holds the hose onto the evacuation probe. Make sure that the clamp is not in contact with the two screws or terminals on the evacuation probe. Move the clamp enough to clear the terminals and retighten it.

b. Inspect the evacuation probe for a faulty installation. The screw heads should be at a 45° angle to the pavement, with the yellow wire at the top. If a faulty installation is discovered, simply turn the evacuation probe by hand, making certain that the probe is firmly planted in its rubber grommet.

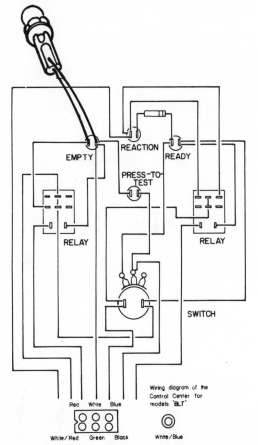

Testing the empty light bulb (Courtesy of Thermasan Corp.)

c. Inspect the yellow lead, which runs from the evacuation probe to the level control module, for a possible short to ground. Remove the yellow lead from the terminal. The empty light should come on. If it doesn't the level control module must be replaced. See "Installation Instructions" for details.

d. Drain the holding tank. Separate the nut from its mating part on the evacuation probe. Inspect the two screws inside the probe fitting for anything which might be contacting them. Reassemble the unit.

e. Inspect the control center module for a loose connection at the light or a burned out bulb. To remove the bulb it is necessary to remove the setscrew from the side of the control center base. Pull the control center off the base, then separate the housing from the bezel. Replace the bulb if necessary.

f. If after checking all of the above, the empty light still will not appear, either the switch or the relay is at fault and a new control center must be installed.

Problem

11. The empty light does not go off.

Remedy

a. This is the normal operating condition of the system when the level of the holding tank is below the probe. This indicates that no more waste is available for pumping and the system should be turned off. Your tank is never pumped dry. If the light is on and visual inspection of the tank indicates it is full, then: (a) Inspect the black and yellow connections to the evacuation probe. (b) Test for a possible defective level indicator module. Remove the yellow lead to the evacuation probe. Insert a terminal or wire and touch it to the screw head of the black wire. If the light remains on, replace the level indicator module. See "Installation Instructions" for replacement information.

ODORS

Problem

1. Odors are noticeable inside the coach.

Remedy

a. Investigate for dry traps in the sink or bathroom. Use Aqua-Kem® or other chemical odor control as instructed. This odor does not necessarily indicate a malfunction of your Thermasan.

Problem

2. Odors are noticeable outside the vehicle after operating the Thermasan.

Remedy

a. Visually inspect the exhaust pipe at the point of waste injection for waste dripping on the exhaust pipe. If the leak is at the hose and Sanijector junction, reclamp the hose at that point. If the leak is at the Sanijector, remove the Sanijector by loosen-ing the two large clamps. Replace the asbestos gaskets and replace the clamp.

Problem

3. Residual odors at the tailpipe.

Remedy

a. Inspect the metering injection assembly for your model number. If the wrong metering injection assembly has been installed, remove the dust cover from the back of the motor by removing the two screws that hold it in position, and install the correct unit.

b. If the proper metering injection assembly has been installed, use AquaSan® for exhaust emission odor control.

6 · Electrical and Refrigeration

The Electrical System

In the past, the camper electrical system often consisted of two separate systems: a 12 volt DC system and a 110 volt AC system.

In recent years most campers have gone to the uni-volt system. This changes 110 volt AC current to 12 volt DC current by means of rectifiers and a transformer. This system allows only 12 volt appliances to be used. On the other systems, some outlets carried 12 volt DC current while others carried 110 volt AC.

NOTE: *Some interior outlets may carry 110 AC current for appliances which cannot be run on 12 volt DC.*

SYSTEM CONTROL PANEL

It is important to know the location of the control panel or the fuse box. Since there is a variety of fused systems used in slide-in and chassis-mount campers, it is wise to consult your owner's manual for exact location. It is important to note which fuse controls each camper component. Place a small tag near each fuse to label it.

Newer campers use switch type circuit breakers which, when the circuit is overloaded, will trip and move to the OFF po-

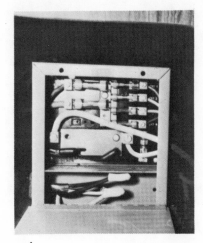

Fuse panel

sition. The switch can be energized by moving it to the ON position. Older units usually use the conventional fuse circuit breaker which must be replaced when it is blown.

CAMPER ELECTRICAL CONNECTION

A trailer park can usually supply your camper with electricity for a small fee. Most camper units have built-in electrical connections which will accept the three-prong electrical connection common to all trailer parks and camping sites. This type of plug is important since it contains an internal ground wire which is necessary

Camper electrical connection

Outside connection to run external components from camper electricity

for camper safety. *Do not* use any connections which do not have this wire.

WIRING DIAGRAMS

Most owner's manuals contain detailed wiring diagrams which include wire color coding and location. It is a good practice to have a copy of this diagram in the

trailer at all times as it makes tracing a particular wire much easier.

The newer campers are engineered so that all the electrical connections are accessible. There are no connections within the camper walls. However, if any structural damage to the camper occurs the electrical lines through the camper skin should be checked.

REFRIGERATOR

The refrigeration unit in either the slide-in or chassis-mount campers can be one of four types: an ice chest type, a gas-fired absorption type, an electrically heated absorption type, or an electric compressor type that operates in the same manner as an air conditioner.

The ice chest type is an insulated compartment that is built into the cabinet structure of the kitchen section. It is sealed with rubber and the inside surface is lined

Typical gas refrigerator

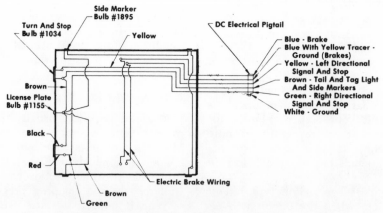

Electrical system diagram (Courtesy of Coleman Corp.)

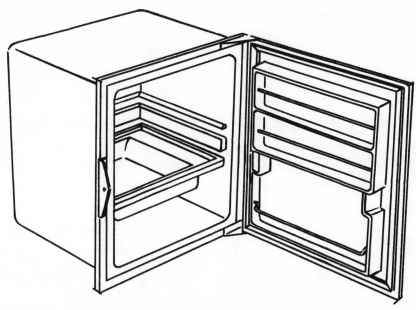

Ice chest type refrigerator

with plastic. The insulation is located between the outer and inner shells. Ice is placed in the unit along with the items to be chilled and the rubber sealing of the door protects the inside from warm air leaks.

The main drawbacks of this system are obvious. The ice melts in time and must be replenished. The water created by the melting ice has to be drained often unless there is an automatic drain tube. And it is impossible to freeze food or keep it frozen in an ice chest unit.

The gas-fired absorption type refrigerator is the most popular type for camper units. It operates from the propane gas system which supplies the stove, oven, hot water heater and furnace. It is compact, clean, quiet, and works very efficiently. The system uses gravity to operate, eliminating the need for any compressors, expansion valves, or capillary tubes. Since gravity is so important to the working of the refrigerator, it MUST be level when working. The flow of the refrigerant will otherwise be restricted and the unit will not cool (see "leveling procedure").

In an absorption refrigerator, the refrigerant, ammonia, boils in the evaporator and condenses in the condenser, just as in the mechanical cycle of an air conditioner. However, pressure is not the only factor that changes the boiling point. The ammonia is exposed to hydrogen, thereby lowering the boiling point. The solution evaporates, which removes heat from the refrigeration compartment. The mixture of the hydrogen and ammonia gases enters the absorber chamber which contains water. Water has a high affinity for ammonia but does not attract the hydrogen. The attraction is sufficient for the water to separate the ammonia from the hydrogen and allow the ammonia to be removed in liquid form.

The hydrogen gas, being much lighter than the ammonia-water mixture, then returns to the evaporator. Now, the ammonia must be separated from the water if it is to be recovered and reused in the evaporator. The solution of water and ammonia flows into a boiler, known as the generator. A gas flame heats the solution in the generator until the ammonia evaporates and separates from the water. The ammonia rises through a tube, which is similar to a coffee percolator, into a separator. This separator is known as a rectifier. Here, the water, which is heavier than the ammonia, is allowed to separate and drain back to the absorber. On the way, it passes through its own section of the condenser and is cooled so that it will more readily absorb the ammonia. The ammonia gas, being lighter, leaves the rectifier through a pipe leading from the top and passes through the con-

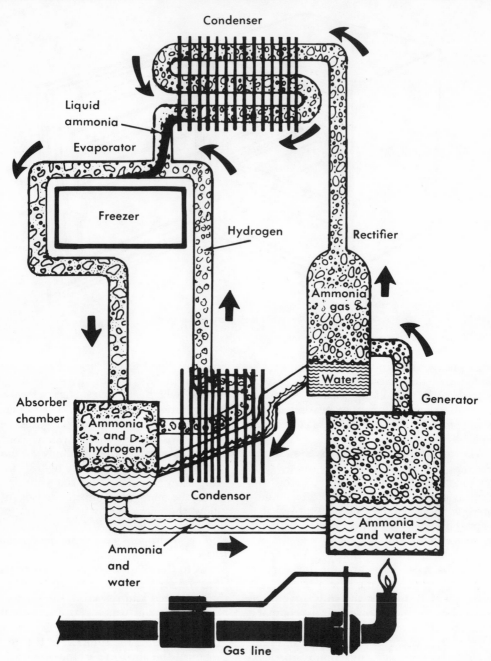

Condenser

Liquid
ammonia

Evaporator

Freezer

Hydrogen

Rectifier

Ammonia
gas

Water

Generator

Absorber
chamber

Ammonia
and
hydrogen

Condensor

Ammonia
and water

Ammonia
and
water

Gas line

Internal workings of a refrigerator

denser, where the heat picked up in the generator is removed. The ammonia gas condenses on its way back to the evaporator.

Thus, it is the exposure to hydrogen in the evaporator and the exposure to the water in the absorber that permits the ammonia to boil and later be condensed. Heat applied to the ammonia-water solution provides the energy to separate the ammonia from the water and make the refrigerant reusable.

If you have an electric absorption type refrigerator, the only difference between the one you have and the one described above is that the heating element is electric rather than a gas flame. These are known to be more trouble free than the gas heated refrigerators because of the fewer operating parts and the absence of a

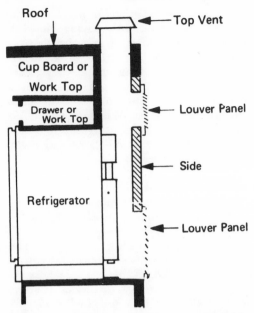

Roof

Top Vent

Cup Board or Work Top

Louver Panel

Drawer or Work Top

Side

Refrigerator

Louver Panel

Refrigerator venting system (Courtesy of Frigiking Corp.)

flame. Gas heated units, however, have the advantage of not requiring electrical connections.

Electrical compressor types operate in exactly the same way that an air conditioner works. The only difference is the absence of a blower that circulates air over the evaporator.

Gas Refrigerator Problems

The most frequent trouble with gas refrigerators is the pilot blowing out. Since the system has a thermocouple, the entire

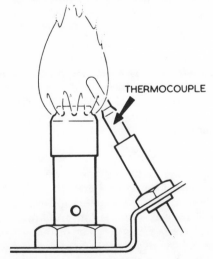

THERMOCOUPLE

Thermocouple location (Courtesy of Frigiking Corp.)

gas supply to the refrigerator is turned off when the pilot goes out. When the pilot fails to supply sufficient heat to the thermocouple, a gas valve closes by means of a thermo-element which expands and contracts with the application of heat. If this occurs, try to light the pilot again by pushing down the button (usually red) on the controller and lighting the pilot with a match or a lighting device. Keep the button depressed for about a minute, allowing the thermocouple sufficient time to heat up and open the gas valve. The pilot should remain lit when the button is released. If it does not, the thermocouple is defective and should either be replaced or repaired.

Before replacing the thermocouple, check to see if the heat sensor is in the correct position. It should be in the middle of the pilot flame. If it is not, adjust it so that the end of the sensor is positioned in the center of the flame.

Pilot Flame Adjustment

Only older units have adjustable pilots while newer models use the fixed pilot system. The flame should be blue with a yellow tip. If it is totally yellow and is giving off soot and an odor, the flame is not burning properly and on older models it must be adjusted. For adjustment, turn the adjustment screw to increase or decrease the air mixture supplied to the pilot. Adjust so that the flame is blue with a yellow tip.

Newer units have nonadjustable pilots but the burner tip may become clogged causing an insufficient flame. The holes in the tip are very small and could very easily become clogged. DO NOT clean the tip with a piece of wire or any other metal device. It will damage the holes in the tip

CLEAN HERE

CLEAN OR REPLACE

CHECK THREADS FOR DAMAGE

Burner maintenance (Courtesy of Frigiking Corp.)

of the burner jet. Clean the jet in alcohol and blow it dry with compressed air. Lighter fluid is a good substitute for alcohol.

Make sure that the burner is positioned so that it is pointed directly at the flue or chimney and in such a way that the proper amount of air can circulate for complete combustion. Misalignment could cause the flue tube to clog with soot.

Maintenance

The unit should be cleaned at least once every year. It is a relatively simple job but should not be neglected. Remove the baffle plate or the louver door. Remove the flame blow-out guard and disconnect the gas pipeline from the pipe nipple. Be careful not to damage the nut. Remove the pipe nipple, which holds the jet, as a unit. Clean the nipple in alcohol or lighter fluid and blow dry with compressed air. Remember that no metal object is to be in-

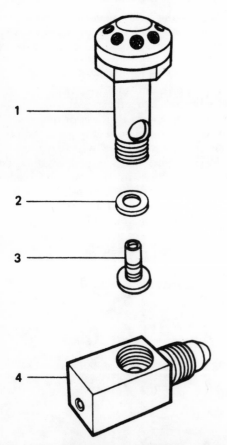

Burner composition (Courtesy of Frigiking Corp.)

1. Burner jet   3. Orifice
2. Orifice ring   4. Burner base

serted into the holes of the jet. Clean the burner tube (generator), paying close attention to the gauze. Use a brush or a cloth and remove any dirt. It is not necessary to remove the burner tube for cleaning. Make certain that the burner jet is covered with a clean cloth so that debris will not clog the jet. When replacing the parts, check for leaks using soapy water. Spread it over the connections and examine for gas bubbles.

CAUTION: *Never use a lighted match to check for leaks.*

The combination of ammonia, water, hydrogen and chromate, which is contained in the system, crystalizes when it contacts air and forms a yellow chromate. This chromate forms around a leak and can be readily identified. If there is a leak in the system do not attempt to service the unit yourself. Take it to a qualified dealer for repair.

Evidence of a leak in the system is a general lack of cooling. The low pressure in the system will cause excessive heat in the absorber coil and lack of cooling.

Leveling the Unit

Since the entire refrigerator system depends on gravity to work, it is imperative that the unit be level at all times. If the refrigerator is not level, this will hamper and possibly stop the circulation of chemicals within the system.

The unit is leveled by placing the leveling device either inside the freezer or refrigerator compartment. Never level the refrigerator by leveling the outside of the cabinet as this will give an incorrect reading.

The leveling of the unit is so critical that it must be leveled to 1° front and back, left and right. If the chemicals are allowed to run in the wrong direction by a tilt of 2 or 3 degrees it could stop the system from working and cause irreparable damage.

Venting the Unit

If you are installing your own refrigerator it should be remembered that after November 15, 1972 the venting laws of the American Gas Association (A.G.A.) must be followed. Consult your dealer for the exact A.G.A. regulations. Roof venting and tight sealing between unit and adjacent cabinets are only a small part of the overall

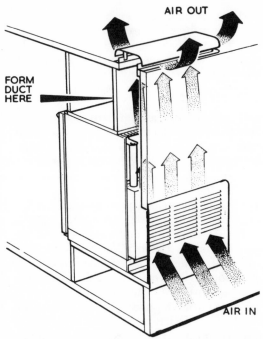

Refrigerator air direction system (Courtesy of Frigiking Corp.)

regulations. These laws were passed to prevent faulty installations which might let burner fumes enter the camper.

One problem in venting is flameout—the pilot flame blowing out while in transit. To stop this, some owners place furnace filters, cardboard and other material over the outside vent. THIS IS EXTREMELY HARMFUL. This restriction will cause the unit to overheat. If this is a problem, turn the unit off while in transit.

Refrigerator Vent

Troubleshooting Chart

Condition	Remedy
The pilot will not light	Check the LP tank to see if it is empty. Look for damaged or blocked gas line.
The pilot goes out when the button is released	Check the thermocouple; it is most likely defective. Make sure that the heat sensor is positioned in the flame properly.
The pilot lights, but the flame is low	The LP gas tank is nearly empty. The refrigerator thermostat is defective and has to be replaced. The burner jets are dirty or clogged and need to be cleaned.
The refrigerator does not cool satisfactorily	There is a restricted vent. Remove any restriction. The refrigerator is not level. The gas bottle is used up. The thermocouple is not being heated properly by the flame. Adjust it or replace it. The burner jet or the burner gauze is clogged. Clean the jet as described in the text. Clean the gauze with a brush. If your unit is designed to have a baffle in the exhaust flue, the problem might lie here. The baffle is designed to distribute heat and cause proper air flow. It may be missing altogether or be installed at the wrong height inside the flue. The gas pressure at the burner is wrong. The burner assembly may not be secured properly and is moving around when the trailer is being towed. The thermostat may be at the wrong setting. Turn it to a higher number. The refrigerating unit may have failed. It is possible that the gases in the unit have become separated and formed a type of "vapor lock." If possible, take the unit out of the cabinet and turn it upside down several times so that the liquid in the boiler can be mixed with the liquid in the absorber vessel. This procedure will restore the liquid balance in the unit.
The refrigerator is too cold	The thermostat is set improperly. Turn the dial to a lower number. There is dirt in the valve of the thermostat. Clean the valve and the valve seat in the thermostat.

This is far better than the damage to the unit which overheating will cause. The crystalized chromate will clog the pump tube, making replacement of the tube necessary.

NOTE: *Should a leak develop in the refrigerator or any other LP gas component, open all the windows and doors in the camper and turn off the gas at the tank. If the leak is severe, evacuate the area to give the gas time to dissipate. Since LP gas is heavier than air it will be most dense near the floor of the camper. Using a broom or a piece of heavy cardboard sweep or fan the gas out the door. This action might look peculiar but it will remove the gas from the vehicle.*

Sometimes minor overheating will cause the separation of water and ammonia. The temperature will not allow both to condense. In the past, units were often physically removed and turned upside down. This served to mix the solution and is called "burping the unit." If this overheating is believed to be the trouble, shut the unit down completely for a few hours. This will cause the chemicals to return to their liquid state. Start the unit to see if it cools. If it does not, it should be examined by a qualified dealer.

GAS STOVES

On adjustable gas stoves, it is important that the pilot orifice, as well as the main burner orifices, are clean to obtain a clean burning flame. If the pilot flame needs adjustment, adjust the pilot air screw to obtain a blue flame with a small yellow tip. The main burners are not adjustable and if kept clean will function correctly.

The fixed burner and pilot models are nonadjustable. If the pilot is not burning correctly, which is indicated by the accumulation of soot, the probable cause is a clogged burner tip. Remove the burner tip and clean it in alcohol to dissolve the blockage. NEVER use wire or other metal objects to open the holes in the tip of the pilot jet. This will damage the orifice. If the blockage cannot be removed by using alcohol, replace the orifice.

Gas stove and hood assembly

7 · Camper Maintenance

Repairs

CANVAS CARE

All canvas equipment must be maintained correctly to prevent rapid deterioration of the fabric.

If the canvas has to be packed when it is still wet, it is important that it be opened as soon as possible and allowed to dry. If this is not done, mold will form on the fabric causing it to rot. If mold or mildew does appear, scrub the spots with soap and water and allow the canvas to dry in direct sunlight. Make certain that the surface is completely dry before packing.

If the canvas starts to leak, either brush or spray waterproofing compound on the leaking area. It is a good practice to apply a double coat to ensure good sealing. The newest sealer on the market comes in an aerosol container which works very well and is easy to apply. These compounds can be found at any well-equipped camping store. The manufacturer's instructions should be followed when applying these sealers.

If the canvas rips, repair it immediately. Rips can and will enlarge.

There are two types of patches available: the conventional sew-on type which works best when applied with a heavy duty sewing machine, and the new iron-on type which can be applied directly to the fabric only with heat. In either case, after the patch has been applied, a coat of water repellent should be applied to both the inside and outside of the canvas. It is a good practice to carry a container of this sealer in the camper.

Whenever canvas is packed, make certain that it will not contact any objects which could cause rips or abrasions.

Canvas without a vinyl outside covering has a tendency to leak when it is touched. If this happens, the only cure is to use spray waterproofing on both sides of the material.

CAUTION: *Guard against placing canvas components under low hanging tree limbs and power lines.*

VINYL CARE

Vinyl is possibly the easiest material to keep clean. Mild soap and water will help retain the original luster for many years. A light clear wax can be used to both shine and preserve the vinyl.

CAUTION: *Cleansers will cause loss of shine and color.*

If vinyl should rip there are repair patches available especially for this material. Follow the instructions with the patch and use some type of sealing compound over the repaired area as insurance against leakage.

ALUMINUM CARE

Some camper units have aluminum sections on their exteriors and interiors. This bright surface keeps the interior of the camper cooler since it reflects heat and the added weight of paint is saved too. Aluminum won't rust and it is also light and reasonably strong.

Cracks may appear in a camper aluminum skin due to road vibration and camper stress. If the crack is small, it can be stopped by "stop drilling." This is done by drilling one hole at each end of the crack with a ³/₃₂ in. twist drill. If the crack is large, the same procedure is used except that a larger crack should be caulked liberally. A doubler plate can be applied over the crack and pop-riveted to the skin. The edges of this plate should be caulked as well.

If the camper is painted, and defects are present in the aluminum or the paint, sand the area removing all paint. Then sand the area using water with low-abrasive waterproof paper. This is done to smooth the edges of the painted surface and is known as "feather edging."

When re-painting the area, use only paint which is made expressly for use on aluminum surfaces. If any other type is used it will peel off in a short time.

Pop Rivets

Pop rivets are used on most aluminum repairs. This type is much easier to install than conventional rivets which must be bucked. The pop rivet gun illustrated is an ordinary type which can be purchased at a good hardware store. Rivets are available in various sizes.

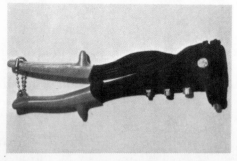

Pop rivet gun (Courtesy of Coleman Corp.)

To use a pop rivet gun, first drill a hole (the same diameter as the rivet) where you wish to place the rivet. Insert the rivet into the gun with the spiked end first. (It is sometimes necessary to lift the handle of the gun when inserting the rivet in order to allow the rivet to catch.) Once the rivet is in the gun, it should stay positioned by itself. The gun is now in the cocked position.

Place the rivet into the hole where it is to be inserted. Press down on the rivet gun and, at the same time, press down on the gun lever. This will compress the rivet and break off its end so it is even with the head. If the end does not break off, open the handle of the rivet gun and take another "bite" on the rivet shaft. Push down on the handle until the end of the shaft breaks. Make certain that the rivet is tight. If it is not it must be drilled out and replaced.

Drilling Solid Rivets

Solid rivets, which are used to hold aluminum panels together, are standard equipment on most campers. If it becomes necessary to remove the panels to gain access to the inner part of the camper or to remove a damaged section, these rivets must be removed. The removal procedure is not as simple as it might seem.

It is important to *take your time* and if at all possible use a variable-speed electric drill.

Drill out solid rivets (Courtesy of Coleman Corp.)

Use a twist drill, of the same diameter as the rivet, and carefully tap a centering mark in the middle of the rivet's head with a center punch and hammer. Place the tip of the drill into this punch mark and start the drill at a very slow speed, applying a reasonable amount of pressure. Be careful

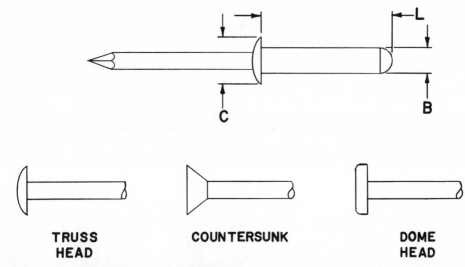

| TRUSS HEAD | COUNTERSUNK | DOME HEAD |

BODY DIA. "B"	HEAD DIA. "C"	HEAD TYPE	LENGTH "L"	GRIP RANGE	HOLE REQ'D.	TYPE
3/16	.342	DOME	.720	.187 − .437	.199	ALUM.
3/16	.336	DOME	.530	.062 − .250	.199	ALUM.
5/32	.255	DOME	.470	.046 − .250	.166	ALUM.
3/16	.625	TRUSS	.656	.250 − .500	.199	ALUM.-GOLD
3/16	.625	TRUSS	11/16	.375 − .500	.199	STL.
1/8	.250	TRUSS	.419	.251 − .312	.129	STL. MAN. ALUM.
5/32	.245	CS	.530	UP TO .312	.166	ALUM.
1/8	.205	CS	15/32	.093 − .250	.136	ALUM.
3/16	.375	BUTTON	25/32	1/2 − 5/8	.199	ALUM.
5/32	.255	DOME	.470	.046 − .250	.166	ALUM.-GOLD
1/8	.215	DOME	.400	.031 − .187	.136	ALUM.-GOLD
3/16	.625	TRUSS	.968	.500 − .781	.199	ALUM.
3/16	.625	TRUSS	.968	.500 − .781	.199	ALUM. DARK

Pop rivet classification chart (Courtesy of Coleman Corp.)

that the drill does not slip from the head and mark the aluminum skin. *Do not drill all the way through the skin.* Drill only far enough to spin the head off the rivet. If you do drill through, you will enlarge the rivet hole and have to use an oversize replacement rivet. Once the head is removed, the remainder of the rivet can be removed from the skin by punching it out with a small drift pin.

Solid rivets are usually replaced with pop rivets for ease of installation. It should be remembered that a pop rivet of ³/₃₂ in. is not equal in strength to a ³/₃₂ in. solid rivet. Check with your dealer for the proper size for replacement pop rivets.

FIBERGLASS REPAIRS

Many campers have fiberglass components which, under the stress of transportation, either crack or break. It is not always necessary to replace the entire section. The following instructions give a detailed outline of how to repair both major and minor fiberglass defects.

Fiberglass repair kits with resin, hardener, thixatrope, fiberglass cloth, and other essentials are available from auto shops which specialize in fiberglass car bodies or boating supply outlets which repair fiberglass boats.

Since both the resin and the spun fiberglass can be irritating to skin, it is important that protective gloves (light plastic type) be worn or that special protective cream be applied to the hands.

If the finished fiberglass has to be sanded, it is important to work in an open area with good ventilation. Use a sander with a vacuum attachment to collect all of the fiberglass dust.

CAUTION: *When working with resin, mix and apply it in a well ventilated area; the fumes can be toxic.*

Minor Repair

For repair of minor damage, remove all paint and other coating from the damaged area. Following directions, mix only enough fiberglass to be used in a half hour. Apply the resin with a rubber squeegee or a putty knife. Fill the damaged area, smoothing the fiberglass to the contour of the panel. Allow to dry and finish by sanding the area and repainting it.

Mixing the resin and hardener (Courtesy of Chevrolet Div. G.M. Corp.)

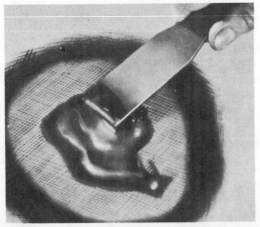

Filling the damaged area with fiberglass (Courtesy Chevrolet Div. G.M. Corp.)

Applying the fiberglass to the fiberglass mat (Courtesy of Chevrolet Div. G.M. Corp.)

Sanding the excess fiberglass (Courtesy of Chevrolet Div. G.M. Corp.)

Major Repair

Completely cracked or broken panels are classified as major repairs. Before mixing the resin in the same manner as for a minor repair, remove all the paint from the area surrounding the damage. Grind the edges of the damaged area so that they form a wide "V." This will provide a good bonding surface for the resin. For severe

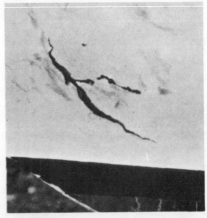

Major repair (Courtesy of Owens-Corning Fiberglas ® Corp.)

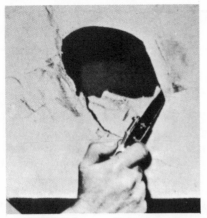

Removing excess damage (Courtesy Owens-Corning Fiberglas Corp.)

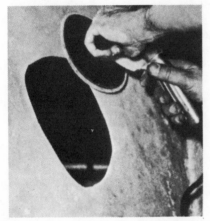

Ruffing the area with a sander (Courtesy of Owens-Corning Fiberglas Corp.)

Reinforcing the damaged area from the inside (Courtesy of Owens-Corning Fiberglas Corp.)

damage, coat a layer of sheet fiberglass in the resin and bond the damaged area on both sides.

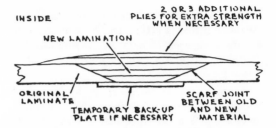

INSIDE — 2 OR 3 ADDITIONAL PLIES FOR EXTRA STRENGTH WHEN NECESSARY — NEW LAMINATION — ORIGINAL LAMINATE — TEMPORARY BACK-UP PLATE IF NECESSARY — SCARF JOINT BETWEEN OLD AND NEW MATERIAL — OUTSIDE

Fiberglas repair construction (Courtesy of Owens-Corning Fiberglas Corp.)

For scratched panels or spot repairs which have not extended into the fiberglass mat, it is necessary to remove the paint from the surrounding area. Feather sand (see "Aluminum Care") the damage with no. 220 or 230 wet sandpaper until it is smooth and even. Do not sand into the fiberglass mesh.

For cracked panels, it is best that the temperature of the work area be at least 70–75° F. This will ensure sufficient hardening of the resin. To be certain of the recommended conditions, check the resin container for the exact instructions. Use lacquer thinner to remove all paint and foreign material from both the surface and the underside of the fractured section. Rough the surface of the fiberglass to create a better bonding surface and remove all jagged edges from the fracture, applying a 30° angle to the broken edges. Align the broken panels. This can be done with C-clamps. Follow the outlined procedures under "Major Repair."

STRENGTH OF THE REPAIR

If the fiberglass repair is done correctly, the finished product will be as strong, or stronger, than the original surface. Extra strength may be added, as explained in the preceding section, by inserting reinforcing panels constructed of mesh fiberglass that have been dipped in the resin solution and applied to the rear of the damage.

Interior Maintenance

Fabric Upholstery: Use a foam cleaner. Soap and water will leave water marks in the fabric.

Carpeting: Most new chassis-mount and

slide-in units use indoor-outdoor carpeting because it needs little care. A small 12 volt vacuum cleaner is a good investment for keeping carpets clean. For stains, use a foam type cleaner.

Vinyl: Use a mild soap and water. Heavy industrial cleaning agents are not necessary. For small spills, a damp cloth will work well.

Drapes: Consult the manufacturer for the recommended cleaning procedure. Some require dry cleaning. Most, however, can be laundered in a conventional washer.

Counter Tops: A mild soap solution will clean tables and counter tops. Never use an abrasive cleaner because it will dull the finish.

Commonsense maintenance of your camper and truck will provide years of trouble-free camping.

Exterior Maintenance

The outside finish of a camper is just as important as the finish of the hauling vehicle. Campers can be washed in the same fashion as trucks. To avoid scratches when using a scrub brush make sure that the camper surface is wet and the brush is dipped in a soapy solution. No harsh cleanser should be used on the camper since the abrasives in it will scratch the finish. Any oil spots can be removed with Naphtha.

CAUTION: *Never use lacquer thinner on any painted surfaces.*

For preserving the finish, use any type of good automotive wax. There are special aluminum cleaning and waxing compounds available for campers with bare aluminum sections.

Appendix

General Conversion Table

Multiply by	To convert	To	
2.54	Inches	Centimeters	.3937
30.48	Feet	Centimeters	.0328
.914	Yards	Meters	1.094
1.609	Miles	Kilometers	.621
.645	Square inches	Square cm.	.155
.836	Square yards	Square meters	1.196
16.39	Cubic inches	Cubic cm.	.061
28.3	Cubic feet	Liters	.0353
.4536	Pounds	Kilograms	2.2045
4.546	Gallons	Liters	.22
.068	Lbs./sq. in. (psi)	Atmospheres	14.7
.138	Foot pounds	Kg. m.	7.23
1.014	H.P. (DIN)	H.P. (SAE)	.9861
——	To obtain	From	Multiply by

Note: 1 cm. equals 10 mm.; 1 mm. equals .0394″.

Conversion—Common Fractions to Decimals and Millimeters

INCHES			INCHES			INCHES		
Common Fractions	Decimal Fractions	Millimeters (approx.)	Common Fractions	Decimal Fractions	Millimeters (approx.)	Common Fractions	Decimal Fractions	Millimeters (approx.)
1/128	.008	0.20	11/32	.344	8.73	43/64	.672	17.07
1/64	.016	0.40	23/64	.359	9.13	11/16	.688	17.46
1/32	.031	0.79	3/8	.375	9.53	45/64	.703	17.86
3/64	.047	1.19	25/64	.391	9.92	23/32	.719	18.26
1/16	.063	1.59	13/32	.406	10.32	47/64	.734	18.65
5/64	.078	1.98	27/64	.422	10.72	3/4	.750	19.05
3/32	.094	2.38	7/16	.438	11.11	49/64	.766	19.45
7/64	.109	2.78	29/64	.453	11.51	25/32	.781	19.84
1/8	.125	3.18	15/32	.469	11.91	51/64	.797	20.24
9/64	.141	3.57	31/64	.484	12.30	13/16	.813	20.64
5/32	.156	3.97	1/2	.500	12.70	53/64	.828	21.03
11/64	.172	4.37	33/64	.516	13.10	27/32	.844	21.43
3/16	.188	4.76	17/32	.531	13.49	55/64	.859	21.83
13/64	.203	5.16	35/64	.547	13.89	7/8	.875	22.23
7/32	.219	5.56	9/16	.563	14.29	57/64	.891	22.62
15/64	.234	5.95	37/64	.578	14.68	29/32	.906	23.02
1/4	.250	6.35	19/32	.594	15.08	59/64	.922	23.42
17/64	.266	6.75	39/64	.609	15.48	15/16	.938	23.81
9/32	.281	7.14	5/8	.625	15.88	61/64	.953	24.21
19/64	.297	7.54	41/64	.641	16.27	31/32	.969	24.61
5/16	.313	7.94	21/32	.656	16.67	63/64	.984	25.00
21/64	.328	8.33						

Conversion—Millimeters to Decimal Inches

mm	inches	mm	inches	mm	inches	mm	inches	mm	inches
1	.039 370	31	1.220 470	61	2.401 570	91	3.582 670	210	8.267 700
2	.078 740	32	1.259 840	62	2.440 940	92	3.622 040	220	8.661 400
3	.118 110	33	1.299 210	63	2.480 310	93	3.661 410	230	9.055 100
4	.157 480	34	1.338 580	64	2.519 680	94	3.700 780	240	9.448 800
5	.196 850	35	1.377 949	65	2.559 050	95	3.740 150	250	9.842 500
6	.236 220	36	1.417 319	66	2.598 420	96	3.779 520	260	10.236 200
7	.275 590	37	1.456 689	67	2.637 790	97	3.818 890	270	10.629 900
8	.314 960	38	1.496 050	68	2.677 160	98	3.858 260	280	11.032 600
9	.354 330	39	1.535 430	69	2.716 530	99	3.897 630	290	11.417 300
10	.393 700	40	1.574 800	70	2.755 900	100	3.937 000	300	11.811 000
11	.433 070	41	1.614 170	71	2.795 270	105	4.133 848	310	12.204 700
12	.472 440	42	1.653 540	72	2.834 640	110	4.330 700	320	12.598 400
13	.511 810	43	1.692 910	73	2.874 010	115	4.527 550	330	12.992 100
14	.551 180	44	1.732 280	74	2.913 380	120	4.724 400	340	13.385 800
15	.590 550	45	1.771 650	75	2.952 750	125	4.921 250	350	13.779 500
16	.629 920	46	1.811 020	76	2.992 120	130	5.118 100	360	14.173 200
17	.669 290	47	1.850 390	77	3.031 490	135	5.314 950	370	14.566 900
18	.708 660	48	1.889 760	78	3.070 860	140	5.511 800	380	14.960 600
19	.748 030	49	1.929 130	79	3.110 230	145	5.708 650	390	15.354 300
20	.787 400	50	1.968 500	80	3.149 600	150	5.905 500	400	15.748 000
21	.826 770	51	2.007 870	81	3.188 970	155	6.102 350	500	19.685 000
22	.866 140	52	2.047 240	82	3.228 340	160	6.299 200	600	23.622 000
23	.905 510	53	2.086 610	83	3.267 710	165	6.496 050	700	27.559 000
24	.944 880	54	2.125 980	84	3.307 080	170	6.692 900	800	31.496 000
25	.984 250	55	2.165 350	85	3.346 450	175	6.889 750	900	35.433 000
26	1.023 620	56	2.204 720	86	3.385 820	180	7.086 600	1000	39.370 000
27	1.062 990	57	2.244 090	87	3.425 190	185	7.283 450	2000	78.740 000
28	1.102 360	58	2.283 460	88	3.464 560	190	7.480 300	3000	118.110 000
29	1.141 730	59	2.322 830	89	3.503 903	195	7.677 150	4000	157.480 000
30	1.181 100	60	2.362 200	90	3.543 300	200	7.874 000	5000	196.850 000

To change decimal millimeters to decimal inches, position the decimal point where desired on either side of the millimeter measurement shown and reset the inches decimal by the same number of digits in the same direction. For example, to convert .001 mm into decimal inches, reset the decimal behind the 1 mm (shown on the chart) to .001; change the decimal inch equivalent (.039″ shown) to .00039″).

Tap Drill Sizes

	National Fine or S.A.E.				National Coarse or U.S.S.	
Screw & Tap Size	Threads Per Inch	Use Drill Number		Screw & Tap Size	Threads Per Inch	Use Drill Number
No. 5	44	37		No. 5	40	39
No. 6	40	33		No. 6	32	36
No. 8	36	29		No. 8	32	29
No. 10	32	21		No. 10	24	25
No. 12	28	15		No. 12	24	17
1/4	28	3		1/4	20	8
5/16	24	1		5/16	18	F
3/8	24	Q		3/8	16	5/16
7/16	20	W		7/16	14	U
1/2	20	29/64		1/2	13	27/64
9/16	18	33/64		9/16	12	31/64
5/8	18	37/64		5/8	11	17/32
3/4	16	11/16		3/4	10	21/32
7/8	14	13/16		7/8	9	49/64
1 1/8	12	1 7/64		1	8	7/8
1 1/4	12	1 11/64		1 1/8	7	63/64
1 1/2	12	1 27/64		1 1/4	7	1 7/64
				1 1/2	6	1 11/32

Decimal Equivalent Size of the Number Drills

Drill No.	Decimal Equivalent	Drill No.	Decimal Equivalent	Drill No.	Decimal Equivalent
80	.0135	53	.0595	26	.1470
79	.0145	52	.0635	25	.1495
78	.0160	51	.0670	24	.1520
77	.0180	50	.0700	23	.1540
76	.0200	49	.0730	22	.1570
75	.0210	48	.0760	21	.1590
74	.0225	47	.0785	20	.1610
73	.0240	46	.0810	19	.1660
72	.0250	45	.0820	18	.1695
71	.0260	44	.0860	17	.1730
70	.0280	43	.0890	16	.1770
69	.0292	42	.0935	15	.1800
68	.0310	41	.0960	14	.1820
67	.0320	40	.0980	13	.1850
66	.0330	39	.0995	12	.1890
65	.0350	38	.1015	11	.1910
64	.0360	37	.1040	10	.1935
63	.0370	36	.1065	9	.1960
62	.0380	35	.1100	8	.1990
61	.0390	34	.1110	7	.2010
60	.0400	33	.1130	6	.2040
59	.0410	32	.1160	5	.2055
58	.0420	31	.1200	4	.2090
57	.0430	30	.1285	3	.2130
56	.0465	29	.1360	2	.2210
55	.0520	28	.1405	1	.2280
54	.0550	27	.1440		

Decimal Equivalent Size of the Letter Drills

Letter Drill	Decimal Equivalent	Letter Drill	Decimal Equivalent	Letter Drill	Decimal Equivalent
A	.234	J	.277	S	.348
B	.238	K	.281	T	.358
C	.242	L	.290	U	.368
D	.246	M	.295	V	.377
E	.250	N	.302	W	.386
F	.257	O	.316	X	.397
G	.261	P	.323	Y	.404
H	.266	Q	.332	Z	.413
I	.272	R	.339		

ANTI-FREEZE INFORMATION

Freezing and Boiling Points of Solutions
According to Percentage of Alcohol or Ethylene Glycol

Freezing Point of Solution	Alcohol Volume %	Alcohol Solution Boils at	Ethylene Glycol Volume %	Ethylene Glycol Solution Boils at
20°F.	12	196°F.	16	216°F.
10°F.	20	189°F.	25	218°F.
0°F.	27	184°F.	33	220°F.
−10°F.	32	181°F.	39	222°F.
−20°F.	38	178°F.	44	224°F.
−30°F.	42	176°F.	48	225°F.

Note: above boiling points are at sea level. For every 1,000 feet of altitude, boiling points are approximately 2°F. lower than those shown. For every pound of pressure exerted by the pressure cap, the boiling points are approximately 3°F. higher than those shown.

To Increase the Freezing Protection of Anti-Freeze Solutions Already Installed

Cooling System Capacity Quarts	Number of Quarts of ALCOHOL Anti-Freeze Required to Increase Protection													
	From +20°F. to					From +10°F. to					From 0°F. to			
	0°	−10°	−20°	−30°	−40°	0°	−10°	−20°	−30°	−40°	−10°	−20°	−30°	−40°
10	2	2 3/4	3 1/2	4	4 1/2	1	2	2 2/3	3 1/4	3 3/4	1	1 3/4	2 1/2	3
12	2 1/2	3 1/4	4	4 3/4	5 1/4	1 1/4	2 1/4	3	3 3/4	4 1/2	1 1/4	2	2 3/4	3 1/2
14	3	4	4 3/4	5 1/2	6	1 1/2	2 1/2	3 1/2	4 1/2	5	1 1/4	2 1/2	3 1/4	4
16	3 1/4	4 1/2	5 1/2	6 1/4	7	1 3/4	3	4	5	5 3/4	1 1/2	2 3/4	3 3/4	4 3/4
18	3 3/4	5	6	7	7 3/4	2	3 1/4	4 1/2	5 3/4	6 1/2	1 3/4	3	4 1/4	5 1/4
20	4	5 1/2	6 3/4	7 3/4	8 3/4	2	3 1/4	5	6 1/4	7 1/4	1 3/4	3 1/2	4 3/4	5 3/4
22	4 1/2	6	7 1/2	8 1/2	9 1/2	2 1/4	4	5 1/2	6 3/4	8	2	3 3/4	5 1/4	6 1/2
24	5	6 3/4	8	9 1/4	10 1/2	2 1/2	4 1/2	6	7 1/2	8 3/4	2 1/4	4	5 1/2	7
26	5 1/4	7 1/4	8 3/4	10	11 1/4	2 3/4	4 3/4	6 1/2	8	9 1/2	2 1/2	4 1/2	6	7 1/2
28	5 3/4	7 3/4	9 1/2	11	12	3	5 1/4	7	8 3/4	10 1/4	2 1/2	4 3/4	6 1/2	8
30	6	8 1/4	10	11 3/4	13	3	5 1/2	7 1/2	9 1/4	10 3/4	2 3/4	5	7	8 3/4

Test radiator solution with proper tester. Determine from the table the number of quarts of solution to be drawn off from a full cooling system and replace with concentrated anti-freeze, to give the desired increased protection. For example, to increase protection of a 22-quart cooling system containing Alcohol anti-freeze, from +10°F. to −20°F. will require the replacement of 5 1/2 quarts of solution with concentrated anti-freeze.

Cooling System Capacity Quarts	Number of Quarts of ETHYLENE GLYCOL Anti-Freeze Required to Increase Protection													
	From +20°F. to					From +10°F. to					From 0°F. to			
	0°	−10°	−20°	−30°	−40°	0°	−10°	−20°	−30°	−40°	−10°	−20°	−30°	−40°
10	1 3/4	2 1/4	3	3 1/2	3 3/4	3/4	1 1/2	2 1/4	2 3/4	3 1/4	3/4	1 1/2	2	2 1/2
12	2	2 3/4	3 1/2	4	4 1/2	1	1 3/4	2 1/2	3 1/4	3 3/4	1	1 3/4	2 1/2	3 1/4
14	2 1/4	3 1/4	4	4 3/4	5 1/2	1 1/4	2	3	3 3/4	4 1/2	1	2	3	3 1/2
16	2 1/2	3 1/2	4 1/2	5 1/4	6	1 1/4	2 1/2	3 1/2	4 1/4	5 1/4	1 1/4	2 1/4	3 1/4	4
18	3	4	5	6	7	1 1/2	2 3/4	4	5	5 3/4	1 1/2	2 1/2	3 3/4	4 3/4
20	3 1/4	4 1/2	5 3/4	6 3/4	7 1/2	1 3/4	3	4 1/4	5 1/2	6 1/2	1 1/2	2 3/4	4 1/4	5 1/4
22	3 1/2	5	6 1/4	7 1/4	8 1/4	1 3/4	3 1/4	4 3/4	6	7 1/4	1 3/4	3 1/4	4 1/2	5 1/2
24	4	5 1/2	7	8	9	2	3 1/2	5	6 1/2	7 1/2	1 3/4	3 1/2	5	6
26	4 1/4	6	7 1/2	8 3/4	10	2	4	5 1/2	7	8 1/4	2	3 3/4	5 1/2	6 3/4
28	4 1/2	6 1/4	8	9 1/2	10 1/2	2 1/4	4 1/4	6	7 1/2	9	2	4	5 3/4	7 1/4
30	5	6 3/4	8 1/2	10	11 1/2	2 1/2	4 1/2	6 1/2	8	9 1/2	2 1/4	4 1/4	6 1/4	7 3/4

Test radiator solution with proper hydrometer. Determine from the table the number of quarts of solution to be drawn off from a full cooling system and replace with undiluted anti-freeze, to give the desired increased protection. For example, to increase protection of a 22-quart cooling system containing Ethylene Glycol (permanent type) anti-freeze, from +20°F. to −20°F. will require the replacement of 6 1/4 quarts of solution with undiluted anti-freeze.

ANTI-FREEZE CHART

Temperatures Shown in Degrees Fahrenheit
+32 is Freezing

Quarts of ALCOHOL Needed for Protection to Temperatures Shown Below

Cooling System Capacity Quarts	1	2	3	4	5	6	7	8	9	10	11	12	13
10	+23°	+11°	− 5°	−27°									
11	+25	+13	0	−18	−40°								
12		+15	+ 3	−12	−31								
13		+17	+ 7	− 7	−23								
14		+19	+ 9	− 3	−17	−34°							
15		+20	+11	+ 1	−12	−27							
16		+21	+13	+ 3	− 8	−21	−36°						
17		+22	+16	+ 6	− 4	−16	−29						
18		+23	+17	+ 8	− 1	−12	−25	−38°					
19		+24	+17	+ 9	+ 2	− 8	−21	−32					
20			+18	+11	+ 4	− 5	−16	−27	−39°				
21			+19	+12	+ 5	− 3	−12	−22	−34				
22			+20	+14	+ 7	0	− 9	−18	−29	−40°			
23			+21	+15	+ 8	+ 2	− 7	−15	−25	−36°			
24			+21	+16	+10	+ 4	− 4	−12	−21	−31			
25			+22	+17	+11	+ 6	− 2	− 9	−18	−27	−37°		
26			+22	+17	+12	+ 7	+ 1	− 7	−14	−23	−32		
27			+23	+18	+13	+ 8	+ 3	− 5	−12	−20	−28	−39°	
28			+23	+19	+14	+ 9	+ 4	− 3	− 9	−17	−25	−34	
29			+24	+19	+15	+10	+ 6	− 1	− 7	−15	−22	−30	−39°
30			+24	+20	+16	+11	+ 7	+ 1	− 5	−12	−19	−27	−35

+ Figures are above Zero, but below Freezing.

− Figures are below Zero. Also below Freezing.

Quarts of ETHYLENE GLYCOL Needed for Protection to Temperatures Shown Below

Cooling System Capacity Quarts	1	2	3	4	5	6	7	8	9	10	11	12	13	14
10	+24°	+16°	+ 4°	−12°	−34°	−62°								
11	+25	+18	+ 8	− 6	−23	−47								
12	+26	+19	+10	0	−15	−34	−57°							
13	+27	+21	+13	+ 3	− 9	−25	−45							
14			+15	+ 6	− 5	−18	−34							
15			+16	+ 8	0	−12	−26							
16			+17	+10	+ 2	− 8	−19	−34	−52°					
17			+18	+12	+ 5	− 4	−14	−27	−42					
18			+19	+14	+ 7	0	−10	−21	−34	−50°				
19			+20	+15	+ 9	+ 2	− 7	−16	−28	−42				
20				+16	+10	+ 4	− 3	−12	−22	−34	−48°			
21				+17	+12	+ 6	0	− 9	−17	−28	−41			
22				+18	+13	+ 8	+ 2	− 6	−14	−23	−34	−47°		
23				+19	+14	+ 9	+ 4	− 3	−10	−19	−29	−40		
24				+19	+15	+10	+ 5	0	− 8	−15	−23	−34	−46°	
25				+20	+16	+12	+ 7	+ 1	− 5	−12	−20	−29	−40	−50°
26					+17	+13	+ 8	+`3	− 3	− 9	−16	−25	−34	−44
27					+18	+14	+ 9	+ 5	− 1	− 7	−13	−21	−29	−39
28					+18	+15	+10	+ 6	+ 1	− 5	−11	−18	−25	−34
29					+19	+16	+12	+ 7	+ 2	− 3	− 8	−15	−22	−29
30					+20	+17	+13	+ 8	+ 4	− 1	− 6	−12	−18	−25

For capacities over 30 quarts divide true capacity by 3. Find quarts Anti-Freeze for the ⅓ and multiply by 3 for quarts to add.

For capacities under 10 quarts multiply true capacity by 3. Find quarts Anti-Freeze for the tripled volume and divide by 3 for quarts to add.